ALSO BY LAURA KIPNIS

Unwanted Advances: Sexual Paranoia Comes to Campus

Men: Notes from an Ongoing Investigation

How to Become a Scandal: Adventures in Bad Behavior

The Female Thing: Dirt, Envy, Sex, Vulnerability

Against Love: A Polemic

*Bound and Gagged: Pornography and the
Politics of Fantasy in America*

Ecstasy Unlimited: On Sex, Capital, Gender, and Aesthetics

LOVE IN THE TIME
OF CONTAGION

LOVE IN THE TIME OF CONTAGION

A DIAGNOSIS

Laura Kipnis

Pantheon Books, New York

Pantheon Books and colophon are registered
trademarks of Penguin Random House LLC.

Library of Congress Cataloging-in-Publication Data
Name: Kipnis, Laura, author.
Title: Love in the time of contagion : a diagnosis / Laura Kipnis.
Description: First edition. New York : Pantheon Books, 2022
Identifiers: LCCN 2021025766. ISBN 9780593316283 (hardcover)
ISBN 9780593316290 (ebook)
Subjects: LCSH: Love—History—21st century. Sex—History—
21st century. Dating (Social customs)—History—
21st century. COVID-19 Pandemic, 2020–
Classification: LCC HQ801 .K559 2022 | DDC 306.73—dc23
LC record available at lccn.loc.gov/2021025766

www.pantheonbooks.com

Jacket illustration: Cupid © P.S. Art-Design-Studio / Shutterstock
Jacket design by Linda Huang

Printed in the United States of America
First Edition
2 4 6 8 9 7 5 3 1

To J.

What is it that I especially find unendurable?
That I cannot cope with, that makes me choke and faint?
Bad air! Bad air!

—Friedrich Nietzsche, *On the Genealogy of Morals*

CONTENTS

LOVE IN THE TIME
OF CONTAGION

LOVE AND EXTINCTION

If you're reading this you recently survived a massive world-wide extinction event, congratulations. Too many didn't. Have a nice big helping of residual simmering rage (so great for the immune system!) at being abandoned by our "leaders," at the profiteers and incompetents and liars, at a cleverly murderous microscopic entity that wants to exploit you as a host and strip your organs for parts. Along with the grief about everything that was lost. About everyone who was lost.

On another but not entirely unrelated subject, how's your love life? No doubt living through an extended planetary contagion will be infecting our relation to other people's bodies and droplets for years or decades to come. A deadly virus alters your sense of what gets transmitted between people and what threats they pose, probably long after the pathogen itself gets beaten down (and apparently we're not getting back to status quo existence anytime soon). Will the cultural afterlife of COVID-19 be as enduring as the long afterlife of AIDS, which reshaped consciousness about sex, love, and body fluids for decades, well after the HIV virus itself was subdued by medical science and a generation of new antiretroviral drugs made AIDS a chronic disease instead of a fatal one? As everyone not insane is hoping the new COVID vaccines will likewise do, fiendish mutations notwithstanding.

But it's not just viruses that mutate, so do we. Our emotions mutate, our relationships mutate. Maybe our ideas about love and what we need or can realistically give another person have mutated. We're different than we were before, including at the cellular level. We're cohabiting with something malevolent—for how long? Everything important is uncertain. How much that shifts the interpersonal calculus is another of the unknowns: we live our lives in profile, we're always catching up to ourselves, violent emotions descend from nowhere derailing you (they call it trauma)—but sure, let's hope and pray that herd immunity and mass vaccinations will make life "normal" again, leaving just the political fractures and cultural hatreds and economic carnage to deal with.

History will obviously have more to say on these subjects, though what may not make it into the official record is how seemingly non-intimate public events—a sociopathic president, the imminent threat of infrastructural collapse—seep into your actual intimacies like runoff from a backed-up sewer, or that the imperiled condition of liberal democracy might mean that if it were ever possible to sustain a deep human connection between two individuals (a balancing act between intimacy and disgust in the best of times), feeling expendable isn't especially conducive to the enterprise. It has ripple effects. It's not as though love takes place in a bubble. To put it in social science-y language: "partnered bonding behaviors" along with "solo and partnered sexual behaviors" were not unaffected, even if you didn't contract the actual disease. Factor in the residual symptoms for those who did. Factor in the economic hits, the loneliness (two-thirds of people said they felt more lonely, coupled or not), the protracted homeschooling ordeals and magnified household neurosis, or fill in your own particulars here.

Is it only me or is there a lingering sense that other people feel, well . . . more encroaching than they used to, even post-vaccination? Just seeing news photos of milling unmasked strangers still gives the risk-averse agita. Do you find yourself recoiling from nearness, in public of course, but maybe in private too? It's not just that other people's variant-laden "aerosolized respiratory particles" might waft your way right as you're inhaling, but once you committed to washing your hands a dozen times a day, now you're a handwasher, right? It's an ontological state, an internal *cordon sanitaire*. Women turned out to be more dedicated handwashers than men, by the way—gender is so insidious.

Back when the virus hit and shutdown commenced, maybe you were coupled, maybe flying solo, maybe some covert or indecisive combination of the two, but when the music stopped we were all face-to-face with our romantic choices and compromises, like it or not. If solo, say hello to the voices in your head, you and they were going to be spending a lot of time together. For those who couldn't endure that prospect there were improvised domestic pods and ad hoc "polycules," platonic and otherwise. If previously coupled, say hello to your emotional bargains, in fact say hello to them twenty-four hours a fucking day, since 80 percent of the global workforce were furloughed or working at home. Anxieties and needs were ramped way up, often taking peculiar forms. A friend's partner insisted on washing the lettuce with soap for a solid year, despite every new finding that "fomite transmission" was not a thing. Okay sure, lettuce has to be washed, but does it have to be washed with soap? Doesn't it taste like soap no matter how much you rinse it? I wondered if the partner unconsciously wished to wash my friend's mouth out with soap, and about all the other subterranean forms of interpersonal violence "the novel coronavirus" was providing cover for. What's a rational precaution, what's an irrational bulwark against the unknown, and what's a thin excuse for payback? Wouldn't lettuce washed with soap taste like a reprimand disguised as a salad? Like your contempt for me on a plate?

It's in the nature of a plague that everything becomes allegorical; as in the Middle Ages, so too in the COVID years. There was so much to interpret: so many data points, so many fault lines, love foremost among them, whether you clung to it, quested for it, or just gave up. Humans invariably

represent what's invisible—love, pain, evil, death—in pictur-
able ways, said C. S. Lewis. Freud called it displacement: why
do we argue about how the dishwasher is loaded when the
real outrage is that there's been no sex for a month? (See his
chapter on dishwasher-loading arguments in *Cascade and Its
Relation to the Unconscious.*)

Let's say you'd previously done the best you could at the
coupling enterprise, balancing the loved one's charms and
solaces against their annoyances on an inner spreadsheet,
engineering togetherness-regulation by means of "busy
lives"—demanding jobs and hobbies and workouts, energetic
socializing, kids, travel, maybe the occasional fling/flirtation/
online dalliance—along with couples therapy as required (if
affordable). Sometimes polyamory worked, refreshed things.
Or swinging—even evangelicals are doing it these days! Also
"throuples." Whatever the geometry, every couple is a finely
tuned calibration of ambivalence and commitment, and
whatever jerry-rigged solutions you'd previously engineered,
COVID scrambled them, scrambled open marriages and
secret trysts—if you'd been stepping out you'd better step
back in, leaving distraught third parties to fend for themselves, as more than a few took to print to publicly complain
about. (*"We were planning a new life together. Now our only
contact is a snatched phone call during his daily run."*) So
long to work spouses and other supplements: all respites
were going to be virtual at best if you had any compunctions,

though maybe not everyone did (the adultery site Ashley Madison reported an immediate spike in new users during lockdown months).

Against the backdrop of sirens and existential dread, you were shuttered with your own and possibly another person's "coping mechanisms." This could be revelatory, and not always in the good way. It turns out that sequestration for months on end amplifies people's (and okay, your own) *habits of personality,* not to mention their actual sound effects, all of which advertise to a sometimes-unbearable degree the biologic and acoustic facts of domestic intimacy. When *The New York Times* ran one of its periodic updates on the state of coupled relations under quarantine (everyone was dying to know how other people were managing the unmanageable), it was quite a cacophony. "If I never have to hear my beloved husband on speaker phone again after this it will be too soon. And let's not even discuss the sound he makes while drinking iced coffee . . ." Or "When spouse's chewing sounds like the tell-tale heart gnashing beneath the floorboards, and my sentences become increasingly punctuated by curses, it's time for serious thinking . . ." A sizable cohort of otherwise loving couples appeared to be growing seriously repelled by their mates under confined conditions.

In addition to the decibels, you were impounded with your mate's (and okay, your own) particular forms of character-ological stuckness, like *No Exit* minus the nympho. (Or the lesbian. Or the impotent guy.) Wow, there are so many ways that people's inner lives just refuse to budge, so many ways that we use each other as convenient projection screens, as showcased in the rotelike repetition of domestic argumentation: the "who did what to whom" argument; the "why did you say x" argument; the "tone of voice" argument; the "you always" argument; the "you said you'd" argument; the "we already discussed that" argument. The "you're not talking about me you're talking about your mother" stratagem. The endless intractable little habits and compulsions, the hamster wheel of ancient calcified wounds and grudges—it's almost like there's some buried streak of deadness at the core of every living human psyche, getting a head start on the mortality thing.

Yet what is it to actually *be alive* was a question the nefarious virus put on the table. The anti-maskers had an answer—life behind a mask was no life. Lockdown was no life. It turns out that viruses themselves are dead but not entirely dead, which is something I hadn't previously known (we're all amateur epidemiologists now). Well, scientists don't actually agree—it depends what you mean by life, they say authoritatively. Viruses are just deeply weird entities, it emerges. Unlike bacteria, which are at least self-sufficient, they're entirely dependent on whomever they invade, and can only reproduce *in coupled states,* by manipulating an unwitting host and coopting the cellular machinery of a more complex creature. Like codependent mates, they're also quite conniving, having evolved spikelike proteins which latch on to the human host cells, allowing them to take over and do whatever they please with you.

You almost have to respect a microscopic entity that baffles everyone to such a degree, brings the entire world to its knees. Indeed, everyone was now talking about the evil new virus as if it had a personality; anthropomorphizing it. It was more intelligent than other viruses, very canny in fact (the long infection window, the asymptomatic transmission), it was efficient and adaptable—it sounded like someone you'd hire to run a company or want to date. Though it soon became clear what an opportunist it was, how adept at taking the shape of the societies it descended on, mirroring us to ourselves. Not just a disease, also a master diagnostician. "The nature of our society is such that we are prevented from knowing who we are," said Ralph Ellison, and kudos to COVID, for patiently explaining things to us, like a hostile shrink. If it didn't kill you, it interpreted you. It took things away, just to see how you'd cope: your social life, your toilet paper, your necessary distractions. It supplied worse things, like doom scrolling. There was a new lab-rat quality to daily life, we were being experimented on by something malign. It exploited the already exploited, enriched the wealthy while further impoverishing the poor, mocked the old, killed off people of color at twice the rate of whites, preyed on the obese, who were already preyed on by Big Food and already the butt of shame. A small surprise was that men were more vulnerable than women, but the evidence had been pointing to that for quite a while.

Was the perfidious virus also a crypto-conservative—will it make us more relationally reactionary, as some think HIV did to gay culture, for which legalized marriage rather than the anti-domestic ecstasies of anonymous backroom sex became the signature program? Fear of disease and fear of freedom aren't exactly strange bedfellows. COVID too invited traditionalism, goading us into self-isolating in our pods, re-upping on monogamy, ditching the outside flings. If you were single you were supposed to stop hooking up and fear potentially interesting strangers, close down all ingress routes like a Cistercian nun. Feeling a little pent up? You could always sublimate your animal urges into frenzies of online moral shaming—Twitter was like the Moscow show trials on an hourly basis, a citizen's firing squad. The masked ranted about selfishness, the anti-maskers ranted about freedom; everyone was morally outraged by everyone else. I was outraged about the endless moral outrage and ranted about that.

And what will all this mean for the future of love? Maybe it's worth pondering before the next random pathogenic bat defecates on the next ailing pangolin, or a hot-wired virus escapes from a secret research lab fridge in Wuhan creating another inadvertent bioweapon, or whatever the hell happened (we'll obviously never know).

—

I once wrote a book-length diatribe against love, though as many people subsequently pointed out, it wasn't so much against love as it was a polemic against modern marriage and the confines of domestic coupledom. And about love taking so much "work" these days that it looks like an assembly line, and the forms of mutual surveillance and policing that are the prevailing norms under coupled conditions, where anxiety about the other person's autonomy and what they might do with it (betray you, humiliate you) dictates much of the texture of daily life *á deux*. The chapter called "Domestic Gulags" had a nine-page litany of capricious rules about all the things you're not allowed to do if you're coupled (as reported to me by de facto couple members). Despite a certain sarcastic tone and Molotov cocktail–throwing at love's propagandists, I still maintain that it was actually a deeply romantic book, though what it romanticized were adulterers—a secret underground cabal of domestic saboteurs and freedom fighters, rebelling against domesticity's confinements and carving out illicit spaces of emancipation for the purposes of "playing around." (Note that this was written before cellphones became another appendage, in the dark ages when tracking each other's movements was a far more primitive enterprise, and people could be off the grid for hours at a time without an alarmed partner summoning the authorities.)

At the time I wrote the book I was not myself coupled, though I'd previously done a twelve-year domestic stint and acquired some firsthand expertise. It's probably not the kind of book you could safely write while in a partnered condition. I was however in a position to hear a lot about coupled restlessness—sometimes that position was horizontal—a cackling spy in the house of domestic discontent.

Over the years, I heard from readers around the world who secretly shared this discontent, many of whom had, like the adulterer-outlaws I chronicled, tasted those temporary and illicit freedoms, or if not tasted them personally, at least understood the impulse to simultaneously flee and stay. I hadn't known I was writing something cross-cultural and hadn't been trying to, though of course pair-bonding is a universal phenomenon, even if norms vary in different places and contexts. The point I'd been trying to make was that subverting domestic regulations can be a creatively fulfilling enterprise, and that there were far more social saboteurs and everyday rebels around than we ordinarily credit. (Back then I was fairly utopian about all this.) Many of us are suspicious of unsanctioned universalizing in these enlightened times, and would far rather talk about the things that divide us—race, class, generation, gender, privilege, red states v. blue states—indeed you hear about little else at the moment. I don't want to get all "kumbaya," but maybe furtive coupled discontent is the one thing that truly unites us as a species.

As a registered domesticity-resister, for the last ten or

twelve pre-COVID years my own coupled life had been conducted in a state of contentiously romantic semi-compatibility, in two separate one-bedroom apartments in New York City. One was uptown in Harlem and the other downtown in Chelsea, maybe twenty-five minutes apart on the subway. By mid-March 2020, as COVID cases rose alarmingly in the area, riding the subway felt dicey and New Yorkers were being ordered to shelter in place. The basic options were Alone or Together, so we crammed ourselves into the Harlem (less cramped) one-bedroom for the duration, not knowing how long that would be. At least there were no on-site kids, parents, or animals—our situation wasn't as crowded as others', but it wasn't as though there was room to think, get away from each other, or do anything the other person didn't feel compelled to comment on at length.

From three or four nights a week together, we went to spending seven (or was it ten?) nights and days a week together, working from home, nowhere to go. The streets were ghostlike and cold. "My schedule for today lists a six-hour self-accusatory depression," to borrow from the Philip K. Dick mental health handbook, which fairly approximated my own mental state. Like many other housebound citizens, I embarked on a Sisyphean project of cleaning and organizing, and in a state of industrious mania spent the first weekend on-site reorganizing my boyfriend's bookshelves by subject and subcategory, to the point that I alone now know where any particular book is located. I attacked closets and bathroom cabinets, making some unwelcome and frankly disgusting discoveries.

Another person's psyche is a foreign country, no less than your own obviously, but that's another story. Forcible domestic confinement was like being an anthropologist embedded with some remote indigenous tribe, trying to decipher its barbaric rituals and obscure mythologies. I fear the experience may have deformed me, perhaps for life. Despite having authored a book mocking the strictures of coupled domesticity, I became perversely energetic about, for instance, policing the (increasing) household alcohol consumption because drinking suppresses the immune system (I read) and I didn't want my mate dropping dead of this malignant fucking virus and leaving me alone, a state I used to savor but the prospect of which now felt (against the backdrop of a barely functioning government and a collapsing healthcare system) terrifying. Random field notes from the early days of immersive coupledom: feeling simultaneously comforted by the little domestic routines and imprisoned by the endless neurotic repetition compulsions. The feeling of knowing another person way too well and also not at all. The dread at being chained to the other person's psychological inchoateness, like a concrete block dragging you to the bottom of the Hudson, punctuated by moments of curative grim levity. Dependence vying with distrust. Feeling in equal measures marvelously understood and criminally misidentified. Both less and more alone. "I love you but I can barely stand you," one of us said to the other.

We started referring to each other as cellmates, not unsarcastically. Meanwhile the homicidal virus was sweeping through the actual prisons: a few miles east at Rikers cases were soaring and the real inmates were dying. Even your bitter jokes felt morally repugnant and an occasion for self-recrimination—everywhere you looked were people who had it plenty worse (the ones who had it better having fled the city for their second homes). "At least we have each other," I liked to quip unfunnily when things seemed grimmest, embellished with implied air quotes. Maybe you yourself sheltered in vast amounts of space, with doors that closed and daily flow charts for chore allocation, lucky you. But whatever your circumstances, your old world had vanished and you didn't know for how long, which forced unasked and better avoided questions about love: Can you imagine an unimaginable world with this person? By yourself? Yes? Sort of? Not exactly? Presumably no one had paired up thinking "How will our personality quirks mesh (or fail to) in a bunker?"

What room is there for ambivalence in a global emergency, no matter how essential to your humanity? Couple ambivalence that dared speak its name in a pandemic felt unpatriotic, like black marketeering during wartime. For Christ's sake, they were shoveling bodies into makeshift morgues in Central Park. We were staring down the abyss, and shouldn't you feel lucky to have someone at your side no matter how passive-aggressive or useless-under-pressure they turned out to be, and periodically driving you to daytime drinking or midnight binge-eating. You too were "No Picnic," as you were frequently told, and how lucky to have a witness at close hand recording every semi-caustic remark you'd let slip, that is if they weren't too busy laminating sanitation directives or arguing about whether bleaching groceries might not be appropriate caution in the face of an unplanned early demise for one or both of you. If there's a necessary suspension of disbelief that adheres couple members to one another, vocal ambivalence is the destroyer of that fragile bond, especially in a crisis. It was like: keep that shit to yourself.

As it happened, I was teaching a film class titled "Dystopia Now" via Zoom that spring, a topic I'd presciently selected some months before dystopia actually descended on the planet, back when there was just a cluster of pneumonia cases in Wuhan that I'd paid zero attention to. (Or had some foreboding registered in the back of my brain? I can't say.) Of the films on the syllabus, the stealthily murderous and blind extraterrestrial creatures in John Krasinski's survivalist post-apocalyptic *A Quiet Place* felt ominously parallel to what we were now living through—pernicious unseen things swooping out of the sky and plucking off family members or anyone who dared make a peep. You feared, as with COVID, that the humans were far outmatched by the antagonists. The jump scares in the movie felt like reading the daily obits, your heart suddenly pounding when it was someone you knew or knew of. Krasinski's husband-character at least had the necessary prepper skills to outwit the predators, whereas practicality was not the signature feature of our little homestead. My own mate's scattershot approach to the world in such matters frequently made me want to beat him with a stick. We would not do well with challenges larger than procuring flour (the local bodegas still had it). It turned out that teaching Dystopia was weirdly cheering: there's always one heroic individual who manages to creatively outwit the antagonists of the future, who locates and preserves the one last teensy speck of humanity and freedom. Sometimes the speck is romance or rebellion, sometimes family or imagination or the last pregnant woman on earth—whatever it was I'd find myself choking up in class talking about it, hoping my students didn't notice. I needed to emulate a heroic individual for them, like Clive Owen in *Children of Men* or Yona in *Snowpiercer*, lead them out of the apocalypse and toward some unknown horizon.

Meanwhile, the virus continued to do what viruses do: circulate. Living in Harlem was like a walking public health study of preexisting medical conditions and who precisely is afflicted with them—you didn't need a medical degree to chart the consequences of race and class on anyone's physical well-being. Asthma rates are twice as high in Harlem as they are in the rest of the city, which is linked to unhealthy housing conditions. The people around the neighborhood leaning on beat-up walkers, or limping around on canes and crutches, milling in front of the methadone clinics in the morning or stooped in front of the bodegas self-medicating out of a paper bag in the afternoon, the physically broken people who'd clearly never in their lives gotten adequate healthcare, were invariably Black. Walking down any Central Harlem street the evidence was abundant, if anyone needed convincing, that long before COVID the American healthcare system operated for people who could pay and callously ditched the rest.

Like some viral imp of the perverse, the pandemic was explaining to the country just how disposable we all were, though some demographics were obviously more disposable than others—not just mortal, but throwaways. As any of us may be to our mates too of course, whatever they'd once whispered in your ear while clasping you in the dark and promising they'd never leave. Uncertainty permeated everything. Someone I know was infected by his ex during breakup sex—he claims not to blame her, though I suspect I would. (I'm a blamer.) Now they're sharing the same RNA molecules for life, which will live on inside his cells until his dying day. As intimate as things get short of cannibalism.

COVID made you think about the innumerable ways we're connected and disconnected, in bed or on the streets. Garbage connected us, for instance—what you throw out someone else has to pick up, then truck around from house to house, apartment complex to apartment complex, an invisible web of connections. "All I've been thinking about all week is garbage. I mean, I just can't stop thinking about it," says Ann (Andie MacDowell) to her shrink (Ron Vawter) in *Sex, Lies & Videotape,* which I rewatched twice in early lockdown days. "What kind of thoughts about the garbage?" he asks in typical shrink fashion. A monologue about garbage ensues: she doesn't know what's going to happen with it, we're running out of places to put it, there'd been a stranded refuse barge that nobody would claim . . . The shrink asks what had triggered the garbage obsession and Ann says it started the other night when John, her husband, was taking out the garbage, and he kept spilling things out of the container and she started imagining a garbage can that produces garbage and doesn't stop, it just keeps making more and more garbage and overflowing . . . (Somehow this resonated.)

Clearly the garbage is a way of talking about "something else," which of course turns out to be her marriage—as we learn (before Ann herself learns), her slimy husband is having an affair with her trashy sister, which maybe at some level she knows? Emotional messes, family junk, secrets exposed— the sister's lost earring turns up while Ann's vacuuming *her own bedroom* (gee, how did that get there?), trying to work off her domestic disgruntlements with a round of energetic household sanitizing. As those in confined conditions with limited outlets are sometimes known to do (this may vary by gender).

I'd been thinking a lot about garbage too. Everyone was producing tons more of it during COVID times, while coupled quarantine sometimes felt like its own form of toxic waste—*"You're full of shit." "That's rubbish."* Those with time on their hands were frenziedly cleaning out attics and basements, which was at least some small way of feeling like you had control over your life, while in reality any of us could be struck down at any moment by an invisible yet omnipowerful adversary. The amount of residential garbage spiked 40 percent in some places, between the de-acquisitioning and the re-acquisitioning: the Amazon boxes, the takeout containers, the failed homemade bread-baking experiments. Some localities had to double or triple the number of garbage runs to the same neighborhoods and still couldn't keep up.

And what about the people whose job it was to haul off the residue of other people's enforced domesticity, exposed to all our collective toxicity day after day? A super I talked to said no one had told him about the three COVID cases in the condo building he worked, he'd figured it out from the weeks of hacking coughs behind certain apartment doors. Aside from which, hours of extra unpaid labor were being extracted from him—gallons more recycling, plus all the boozing, the day-drinking for those who'd been laid off and felt worthless, and us working from home and going blind after the tenth Zoom call of the day. I'd noticed the increase in empties on my own floor, some percentage of them ours. Your secret booze problem isn't exactly a secret from your super.

Sanitation workers were in the news because they were testing positive all over the country at alarming rates, and many even dying so our garbage could get picked up. Garbage collection has always been one of the most dangerous jobs around—you can get exposed to hepatitis B and *E. coli,* there's chemical seepage, there are torn bags with hypodermics, glass, razor blades, excrement. . . . With COVID, some amount of trash was obviously coming from infected people, their used tissues and face masks and gloves, upping the risks and stress for those transporting it to its next interim home. They had the stress of not knowing what was in the backwash sloshing around inside the trucks—if there's water in the hopper it's easy to get it in your nose or mouth. They feared bringing it home to their families and not being able to live with themselves if they did. Before there'd been camaraderie on the route, now they dreaded going to work. At the beginning no one was telling them how to protect themselves—they were being treated more than a little like garbage themselves. When summer came I read some suburbanites saying online that they weren't inviting essential workers to their pool parties, though I imagine they still wanted their party trash hauled away by someone.

If the professional sanitation workers were feeling disposable, so were we amateurs, scrubbing ourselves down hourly against unseen threats, Purelling head to toe, interrogating ourselves and our housemates about what we'd breathed or touched. So great for intimacy! Booze consumption doubled, domestic violence went up an estimated 20 percent (no estimates on the percentage of couples who felt like killing each other but refrained), gun sales spiked, and Mary-Kate Olsen filed for an emergency divorce after her husband invited his ex-wife to shelter with them, which she and her fans interpreted as a hostile gesture. In my own household an open can of Diet Coke was thrown. I'm not naming names, I'll just mention that if you're in a blind rage, one minute winding up like Roger Clemens and the next trying to understand why there's fizzy warm liquid streaming down your back, your mental acuity has suffered from too much time indoors and your pitching mechanics need attention. (Men are better at "mental rotation" of three-dimensional objects in space, a skill women reportedly struggle with according to the evo-psych crowd. The other party, with the unfair advantage that accrues to ex-jocks, was sufficiently coordinated to duck the beanball.)

Amid the cleaning frenzies another thing getting disposed of were used-up spouses. Was it having time to actually *talk* to each other that was pushing coupledom to the breaking point? When things initially opened up, divorce lawyers reported a surge of calls from people inquiring about separating, up to 75 percent higher compared to the previous year, said a lawyer in Great Britain; similar upswings were reported around the world. An Australian poll said 42 percent of couples had experienced negative changes in their relationships. An American poll said more than a quarter of adults knew a couple likely to break up. There was an epidemic of dubious polling, along with random lockdown epiphanies: people gazing into the post-COVID future and deciding they were better off going it alone, plotting exit stratagems. Not everyone had that choice—health insurance and finances provided the household cement for plenty of broken couples who'd probably have been better off apart. A year into the pandemic, in spring 2021, new reports said that divorces had slowed—a "reverse-trend," but 34 percent of couples reported increased relationship stress, which was (big surprise) highest among couples whose financial situation worsened.

"Can Your Relationship Survive the Togetherness of a Pandemic? Here Are 11 Things Couples' Therapists Recommend." Even in the first weeks of lockdown, dozens of articles on the fate of love in COVID times were already popping up. Reports were that libido levels had crashed, which probably didn't help anyone's relationship survival prospects—people were upping their antidepressant dosages (no libido boon in the best of circumstances), or maybe the problem was that it was impossible not to think, as you're getting down to business: "What if this is the last time?" as a friend of mine admitted. A guy from the Kinsey Institute explained: "A state of high threat, characterized by stress or anxiety, is not conducive to having sex." We've evolved to have a highly developed disgust response, he said, an innate tendency to avoid things that have the potential for disease transmission, which is why we're grossed out by feces and maggots. Many were likewise turned off by the idea of kissing someone during a pandemic, he concluded.

Was that what was tearing so many couples apart, that your loved one seemed suddenly . . . contaminated? Or potentially? Anxiety loves an anti-bacterial wipe, and I suspect it was the rare charmed twosome who managed to avoid all dissension about sanitation procedures. In fact I'd once clipped a story about such an outlier couple. This was Wayne and Carol Cleghorn—he the manager of a local grocery store, she a registered nurse, living in a middle-class suburb outside of Chicago—whose three-bedroom house was discovered to be crammed full of rotting trash: oozing food remains, bottles, cans, papers, and human excrement, piled so high (at least two feet in places) that walking was impossible. (I've occasionally wondered if reading about the Cleghorns was the inception of my qualms about coupled domesticity, the suspicion that behind closed doors things are really a mess.)

When police investigating reports of a break-in had knocked on the door they'd been hit with an unbearable stench. Wayne, thirty-eight, was home watching TV, nonchalantly eating a snack and somehow oblivious to the mounds of filth and the overwhelming stink. The upstairs toilet was broken and the floors of the master bedroom were knee-deep in mounds of shit. It must have been like entering one of

Dante's circles of Hell, as imagined by Martha Stewart. Later that week city workmen equipped with a forklift, pickaxes, shovels, and gas masks, taking breaks every ten minutes, spent two entire days hauling an estimated three tons of garbage from the house—it had to have been accumulating for years. There was even trash on the bed.

Neighbors were incredulous—"I can't see any reason for something like this," said one. "We have garbage pickup out here twice a week."

I thought about the long-deceased Cleghorns periodically as our trash pile accumulated during the shutdown—what if you just "forget" to take it out, or it's the other person's turn and goddamnit you're sick of doing it yourself again, and it turns into a standoff, one of those gruesome little pacts couples make, a silent arrangement to see just how bad things can get. (Wayne did refer to "marital strain" at his hearing on charges of creating a public nuisance.) One minute you're "nice, sociable people," as a neighbor described them, the next your lives are splattered across the headlines and workers are shoveling your actual shit into dumpsters.

Yes, it's hard to let things go sometimes. Grudges, for example, which litter the domestic landscape like magazines you can't bear to throw away but know you'll never read, and if you're like me (a grudge-collector par excellence) they get piled higher and higher until you have to forge paths between the stacks just to get to the bathroom. "The secret life of grudges," as Adam Phillips puts it. Maybe there's a little

Cleghorn in all of us—obviously making a mess of things is not unknown in the annals of human behavior, and there are so many versions of emotional detritus too. I guess you have to love each other for the mess you are, and hope to be loved in turn, in all your grossness. That undisposed scrum of hair in the tub after your mate takes a bath—intimacy at its most tangible. Isn't every successful couple a private pact, as with the Cleghorns, to ignore certain glaring things?

Someone in the midst of a breakup once said to me, about selecting life mates, that when you first meet someone you're going to be in love with you get this instant glimpse, in the first couple of seconds, of who exactly the person is. Then you get to know them, maybe you even spend years together, and the picture changes and deepens, they're a vast and complicated mystery you'll never get to the bottom of, for better or worse. Sometimes for worse. Then you break up and you realize they're exactly who you'd known they were in that first split-second glimpse, but somehow you forgot what you knew, or didn't quite forget but conspired with yourself to overlook it so that things could proceed. That kept coming back to me. Is it true? I have no idea. I suppose it's a story about blind spots and how we were all sequestered with their consequences, and how (by definition) you don't know where they are in advance until they sneak up and bash you upside the head.

Love carves the world into roles. Classically you have the person who loves more and the person who loves less, the one who acts out and the one who puts out the fires, the one who falls apart and the one who glues back the pieces. Coupledom is organized around capacities and defenses: having shut yourself off from feelings, you seek out an emotive mate, then berate them for their over-emotionality. Or you're a control freak with a mate whose life is in perpetual chaos, which you secretly despise but also keeps you engaged since carping about their irresponsibility is (secretly) a welcome distraction from facing your own problems. All of which COVID ruthlessly exposed or remorselessly accelerated—like maybe you'd affianced yourself to the life of the party and suddenly there's no party, just four walls and Netflix. What now? COVID jettisoned the divertissements, for instance *all the other people* who'd made coupled life sustainable, leaving you face-to-face with: each other.

One theory of coupling is that life is a pharmacist, dispensing mates who balance our weakness and complement our strengths: a realist for every dreamer, a miser for every spendthrift, medicine for your personality deficits. Alternatively, we find mates who bring out the worst in us: a partner is sent by the universe as a character test, to expose what you're really made of. And show you where your "buttons" are—a term I've always despised, it reminds me of supernumerary nipples—like some pernicious infrared sensor, detecting what's most likely to set you off and then invariably "going there." One of you is the criminal, the defiler of proprieties, to the other falls the job of "restoring order"—this was my unfortunate role, having selected a mate who's even more of a scofflaw than am I, thus consigning myself for eternity to the boring job of household cop and resident superego. "The last Puritan," he loved to call me whenever I tried getting him to do some normal adult thing he didn't feel like doing.

At best a couple is a workable neurotic pact, the paradigm being women who marry captured serial killers, getting the thrill of proximity to a dangerous man alongside the satisfaction of seeing him behind bars, castrated by social constraints. Incidentally, there's a term for this: "hybristophilia," which means being aroused by your partner's outrageousness and thrilling to their crimes, while being law-abiding and virtuous yourself. Note that serial killers get tons of fan mail in prison, they don't even have to be good-looking.

"You fell in love with a weirdo," Ted Bundy (Zac Efron) tells his in-the-dark girlfriend in the superbly titled biopic *Extremely Wicked, Shockingly Evil and Vile,* which I watched (possibly more than once) during lockdown. "That makes you weird by association." I was on a serial killer spree myself, but so must everyone in the world be as there's not exactly a shortage of serial killer entertainment to consume, in fact there's quite a glut. "I'm not a bad guy," says Bundy. "I feel like nothing without him," says his girlfriend, before finding out that her taste in men needed some scrutiny. At the real-life Bundy's trial scores of women congregated, describing him as dreamy. Did they thrill to his amorality, get off on it? See him as godlike—God obviously being the original serial killer (as we've all recently witnessed close up) and equally an unstable control freak, according to Jack Miles, God's unflappable biographer (*God: A Biography*). Still, what's this secret erotic residue the serial killer romance leaves smeared on the cultural psyche?

No one ever said the sustainable neurotic pact is without its rough patches. There's always something you have to overlook. I recall trying to explain the concept of the deal breaker when I and my boyfriend were first getting together. He—recently separated, not having dated in a few decades—purported not to grasp the concept, nor that of the "red flag," which I also attempted to explicate. He argued that people aren't Chinese menus, you don't get to choose one item from Category A and so on. That, in his view, the so-called flaws are what make someone alluring and you can't have one without the other. I found this touchingly naïve—he was super-attractive, but clearly needed to be saved from his unworldliness. Little did I realize that I was the witless prey; he'd found an open window and climbed into my bedroom, as Bundy feigned being on crutches to lower the guard of his victims, making them see him as vulnerable—it was his signature "in."

Then there's Morrano, the brilliant and refined eponymous serial killer in *Serial Killer,* another pandemic fave, who traps Agent Younger, the lovely young FBI profiler, in her apartment and proceeds to torment her with his knowledge of her conflicted inner life, while quoting Shakespeare. Serial killers turn out to be oddly adept at intimacy, or that's the fantasy. Naturally she recognizes the quote, because he understands her better than she understands herself. Like it or not, he's her soulmate. Which is obviously what we've all been schooled to desire in a mate—to be truly *known in our essence*. "You have a love of the poets," he tells her appreciatively, like they'd met on OkCupid. The downside of their special rapport, as in all intimacies, is someone "getting into your head." The thrill of being known means being contaminated by the knower's perversities—but isn't this what happens in our deepest connections, isn't that the key to the whole *frisson* of it? That alluring combination of solace and danger?

There's no mystery why "fear of intimacy" is so endemic—what if the Other's intentions are perfidious? What if the beloved is a . . . (fill in the pathogenic personality type of your choice). Once you've been penetrated by intimacy as by a vampire's bite, how will you maintain your boundaries? How to protect your defenseless cells or inner being from spiky roving things that want to invade you, seduce you, bend you to their purposes?

Between the recently acquired expertise in virology, months of forcible cohabitation, and certain unfortunate streaming choices, the amorous world had come to feel far more sinister. At least your serial killer boyfriend isn't trying to reform you, not engaged in some prolonged campaign to

turn you into a better person, unlike the ostensibly less murderous mates.

Other people were reading plague lit for guidance—Boccaccio
and Camus study groups were springing up online—but my
proclivities ran more to the literature of domestic claustro-
phobia and crackup, of which there's no shortage. If you like
your coupled antipathy in an absurdist vein, may I recommend the Romanian-French playwright Eugène Ionesco's
Amédée, or How to Get Rid of It, except that it reads as
almost too uncannily of our moment. This is the story of a
fractious married couple—the husband, Amédée, is a blocked
playwright, his wife, Madeleine, a switchboard operator (I
believe "communication issues" are being signaled)—who
share their Paris apartment with a gigantic corpse that's getting bigger and bigger by the day, especially his finger- and
toenails, which apparently grow faster once you're deceased.
A symbol of their dead love? The neurosis that holds them
together? A former lover of Madeleine's, killed in a jealous
fury by Amédée? (The backstory is murky.)

Formerly confined to the spare bedroom, the corpse has
lately grown so large it's starting to crowd the couple out of
their apartment which, as you'd imagine, does nothing to
improve their day-to-day relationship. Nor does the deadness
of the corpse prevent Amédée from treating it as a rival and

becoming irked about the amount of time Madeleine spends trimming its nails (and who knows what else) when she disappears to its quarters for prolonged closed-door tête-à-têtes, not that Amédée especially wants to hang out with her himself.

A relationship triangulated by a corpse in the spare room had certain resonances with my own current situation. Like life *chez nous,* the two of them argue constantly and their moods are never in sync: when he's up, she's morose, when she calls him "darling" he feigns not to hear, responding maddeningly, "What did you say?" When she accuses him of calling her "stupid," he non-apologizes, "I didn't mean you were stupid. It's just that you're not logical, which isn't the same thing at all." She, in turn, berates him about his writing block (which didn't endear her to me)—he's written only two lines in the fifteen years the corpse has been in residence. Or was it Madeleine's nagging that killed his creativity? I knew how he felt: trying to write in confinement felt about as pleasant as a Corona nasal swab, jabbing and scraping up into your skull through the narrowest of orifices for what feels like a half hour to extract evidence of a possible malady.

Additionally, large poisonous mushrooms are sprouting up between their dining room floorboards—something rotten has definitely overtaken this household. The two of them live in mutually recriminatory isolation, hiding guiltily from their neighbors, and haven't seen friends in fifteen years, but how can they entertain between the corpse and the mushrooms, and the apartment being what it is (despite Madeleine's constant frantic cleaning and scrubbing)?

Like Amédée and Madeleine, we too were guiltily hiding from our neighbors—at least three had come down with the virus, including someone down the hall whose prescriptions we picked up, leaving them outside his door then scurrying away, trying not to inhale. His marriage had recently imploded and his ex had left the country; if we didn't hear from him for a few days I'd start worrying that he was lying dead a dozen yards away—how would we know until he started decomposing?—while simultaneously worrying that extra trips to the store to pick up groceries for him (he'd gone vegan and required backbreaking gallons of oat milk) would kill us. None of us had been accustomed to thinking about the proximity of death on such a daily basis, now it was practically hovering in the next room.

Amédée and Madeleine decide to finally stop squabbling about each other's failings and drown the corpse by throwing it in the river, which is at least something they can do together, like Netflix date night, though of course they squabble about corpse disposal too. The saddest thing is that even when Amédée fleetingly attempts self-transformation in the final scenes, literally taking flight, floating up into the sky like a hot-air balloon, Madeleine's still not done trying to bring him down. He thinks he's finally out of reach of her and her negging, but there she is calling after him, "You may have gone up in the world, but you're not going up in my estimation!" To which he cries plaintively from above, "It's not my fault," a refrain I've heard not infrequently in my own household. When he pleads "Why don't we try to love each other, please, Madeleine? Love puts everything right, you know . . ." I felt moved by his optimism—my mate too is far more upbeat about love's healing properties than I, who prefer my gloom and cynicism.

Why did a playwright and a switchboard operator get together in the first place? Why do any of us? Needless to say, there was plenty of time under quarantine to contemplate your own mate selection procedure, and wonder if you'd have conducted it in the same manner had you been told pandemic times were coming. Were you a practical type with an affinity for a romantic temperament in a partner, drawn, like Madeleine, to troubled souls with self-inflicted wounds and poetic interiority? Had you, like Amédée, sought a mate whose groundedness would ground you too, only to find with the passing of years and receding of libidos that their endless practicality had become stultifying and soul-killing? Had you, like Madeleine, entrusted your well-being to a partner who feels and feels, with feelings as big as the Ritz or Freud's entire *Standard Edition,* which had its enticements in more tranquil times but under this endless fucking confinement was starting to grate on your last nerve? Does your mate's haphazard approach to matters of finance (or conversely, their parsimonious zeal for a bargain) make you want to smack them with a cast-iron skillet?

I suppose it's insensitive to joke about domestic mayhem, but why *is* there such an endless supply of it in popular culture? What a beloved entertainment genre it is! Is it that we secretly know every marriage is a little murder? Every couple the venue for unimaginable potential violence, or at least the emotional variety? To be sure, the theme of imperiled women has long played a starring role in the gothic imagination: there's that familiar couple, The Husband Who Turns Out to Be Not Who You Thought He Was, and his occasional counterpart, The Wife's Revenge. In domestic noir, spouses of every gender are their own kind of pathogen; as soon as you've let down your guard they'll be trying to do you in, often with your own stupid complicity. In some recess of the collective psyche, the person you love is always about to destroy you, a secret sociopath. Especially the husbands—he's cheating on you and everyone in town knows, or he's plotting to murder you—for your money, the insurance, or the comely neighbor—or a thousand variations on the theme of a husband's fundamental unknowability. He's handsome and successful but also a rapist, he killed someone in the past and somehow never mentioned it, he's possessed by a parasitic spirit from The Further and has just killed the medium who was trying to exorcise it while you were out of the room. (In the best domestic horror, it's not the house that's haunted, it's your spouse. Sure, you can try moving, but the daemon is sleeping right next to you. The normal is always *paranormal*.)

Whatever the specifics, domesticity is your funeral. Particularly if you're female. Especially if he seems a little *too* perfect. A little *too* loving. Why has he been so strangely moody lately, what's in that locked drawer in his office, did he really run out of gas when he got home so late the other night, hadn't you filled the tank the day before? Does every husband have nefarious secrets and a secret life? (Yes.) Is every wife about to unravel his lies only to emerge saddened but triumphant? (Probably.) It's not only in gender studies departments that heteronormativity is under attack, try Netflix.

With no social life to speak of these characters were crowding my thoughts at night, a new circle of friends, each with a dire problem. In *The Undoing,* a rich and beautiful woman shrink wakes up and her charmingly handsome doctor husband is gone—she thinks to an out-of-town conference (he's a pediatric oncologist, what could be nobler?), but then he doesn't call and doesn't call, and it turns out she had no idea who she was married to. This was based on the accusatorily titled novel *You Should Have Known,* which of course I also had to read—that "you" is a dagger hiding in a rebuke—only to learn that what "you" should have known is that your spouse (or in my case, spouse equivalent) *is really a stranger.* But doesn't anyone whose spouse betrays or leaves them actually *know all along* what was going on, asks the novel; didn't you know the true character of your future betrayer but collude with yourself to ignore "the signs"?

This was sobering. There are *always signs,* at least that's the conceit. People aren't fundamentally unknowable, you were just epistemologically lazy. Yet given what a double bind knowability turns out to be, who wouldn't resist it? You didn't *want* to read the signs, because what then?

In actual life, the thirtyish friend of a friend, Adele, also awoke one morning a few months into the pandemic to find that Matt, her husband of five years, was gone. Left. And had cleared out exactly half their joint bank accounts ("psychopathically scrupulous" was how she later thought of his math), which included the proceeds from a recent house sale that was supposed to be the down payment for a new house they were bidding on.

The immediate problem was that they'd moved into her parents' basement while house hunting in the area (at the time, more than half those between ages eighteen and twenty-nine were in fact living with their parents, the highest number since the Depression) and though they'd all always been a close unit, now you had four adults working from home, coexisting in pretty tight quarters. A couple of weeks before he split there'd been a big blowup over the house shopping, with Matt not wanting to see a place Adele very much did want to see, and being inexplicably petulant about it, and her mother telling him "You're acting like a child." And Matt shoving

Adele's father and Adele's mother grabbing a fireplace poker saying, "No one shoves my husband," while Adele demanded her mother put the poker down, then getting in between her father and Matt, and Matt saying he was leaving, and the family demanding he stay because there was a pandemic and where was he going to go? He couldn't just go out somewhere, inhale germs, and put them all at risk.

When Adele woke up alone that morning two weeks later, there was an email from Matt. The subject line was a frowny face. He said he'd decided to leave her but had been afraid to tell her in person. Later he elaborated that she always played the debate champion and he could never win an argument, and he was afraid that if they talked in person he'd lose his shit and things would get violent. He needed some space. He needed to breathe.

Had Adele seen it coming? Had there been signs? In a sense—she had all the information, but could only put it together in retrospect. We live forward but understand backward (Kierkegaard). They'd been in couples counseling, it's not like things had been perfect. Later she thought there'd been a seething rage in him she'd never let herself see. He'd been sober for nine years but in the dry-drunk fashion, addicted to AA meetings and self-suppression in ways she later admitted to herself she'd started to find boring. But it was her job to prop him up, assuage his feelings of inadequacy and uselessness, reshape herself in the manner we all do when we're trying to make things "work"—sculpt ourselves into what our mates need us to be. He needed her to be his savior, which was thrilling in the early days, though also deforming. They both had the habit of blaming her for his volatility, meaning that when he acted out, she felt responsible for letting him down. While also having to put up with a lot of drama. I had a sense that what someone else would have regarded as red flags were part of the attraction for her. (She wrote poetry.) Such are the romantic pacts we make.

Had the pandemic caused the split? Well, yes and no, she thought—it exacerbated and brought to light how rotten the marriage had become, in the same way it was exacerbating and bringing to light so much that had been rotten in the country all along. Maybe everyone's marriage had become a metonym for our fatally divided nation, even when you agreed with each other politically. If Matt had been able to leave the house and cool off the night of the big conflagration, would things have eventually settled down? I imagine he must have felt humiliated about losing it in front of her parents—communal living evidently hadn't helped the marriage. He'd spent the following couple of weeks plotting his escape, Adele only later realized—consulting a lawyer, opening a new bank account. She came to feel, bitterly, that he'd chosen a way to leave that would inflict the maximum psychological damage. At the same time, she worried about his well-being, thought about trying to reconcile. She didn't see how she could start over with someone else. It was zombie love, dead and alive at once.

—

Romantically partnered or not, the number of American adults living alone has doubled in the last fifty years, and it's the same story around the developed world. What accounts for this significant modification of housing arrangements? Clearly other people are *increasingly impossible to live with*. But when did they all get so irritating? So prickly and fragile, so quick to feel and express injury? So thin-skinned? Did other people's personalities always get in the way of you trying to love them to this extent, was it always like having to climb through a field of nuclear waste and brambles to get to the sunny spot on the beach?

Note that there was another "epidemic" raging long before COVID (or so said all the experts), another contagious condition: this would be the epidemic of *narcissism*. Which can be defined variously, but let's just specify it as the bedrock of love in our time. Everywhere you go, someone's complaining about someone else's narcissism: everyone's ex is a narcissist, also the last person you met online, and your toxic college friend and probably your mother. Note that *they're* all going on about how narcissistic everyone else is too. It's the air we breathe these days, the air in the room that someone else is taking up with their nonstop suffocating narcissism.

I first started thinking about the bad faith of the narcissism indictment a few years ago when I was out to lunch with a friend. Not any special sort of egomaniac, just someone with the usual ambitions and insecurities, who nevertheless spent *an entire hour* talking about a book she'd written that was about to come out: the editors squabbling over magazine rights, the upcoming book tour, the fabulous early reviews, the national publications clamoring for her new thoughts . . . There were so many *pressures* on her at the moment—feelers about a big job in another city, and she was about to leave the country, and she was being pressured to take over a prestigious administrative post because the person who was supposed to do it had suddenly dropped dead from some sort of embolism . . . Here I spied an opportunity to change the subject, as another writer we'd both seen deliver a talk a few weeks before about *his* new book, someone I knew casually, had himself just a couple of days before suddenly keeled over at a party and never regained consciousness. "Wasn't that what happened to Y?" I interjected, adding the usual clichés about what a shock it was, though in circumstances like these it's never clear whether you're mourning the dead acquaintance or the possibility that something equally gruesome could happen to you next.

My friend brushed away the clichés like so many bothersome insects. "Yeah, yeah," she said. "I hate to speak ill of the recently deceased, but could you believe that talk? What a narcissist!" He kept spouting on about how influential his work had been, my friend complained. She and her seatmate—she named a critic, known for being a smug bitch in print (hearing her name I noticed a bad feeling wafting through the back of my brain—had she once been nasty about something I'd written? I couldn't recall, but felt aggrieved anyway)—had been rolling their eyes the entire time. I thought back. What I remembered about the talk were Y's careful self-deprecations—he seemed to be consciously avoiding touting his own work, which had indeed been influential, though I suppose the deprecations could be ungenerously construed as an index of just how self-important he really was, as if we'd all have been sitting there dripping with envy over his accomplishments if he hadn't deftly deflected it. The point is that even in death, his selfhood impinged on my friend's. Yet I understood her position: to anyone with a book about to be published, the existence of other people's books can only be profoundly wounding. The mere fact that someone other than you is up at the podium speaking feels like—as we now routinely say—a narcissistic injury.

Perhaps in retaliation for the unkindness about Y, who'd been so exuberant and brimming with good spirits and then abruptly chopped down, an evil imp seized my vocal cords and I heard myself intimating that I'd actually been a little frustrated by my friend's new book (she'd given me an advance copy), which seemed to hedge its bets. She tried not to look perturbed though clearly she was desperate for my approval; all the professional adulation in the world was at that moment insufficient. A fracture in her sense of self had opened—there was no ballast there, no continuity. Of course it's not as though these same things don't afflict me too: the finely honed sense of one's own status vis-à-vis others, the propensity for shifting the conversational focus to yourself, the perennial sense of injury. When other people are yabbering on at me about themselves I feel that they simultaneously want my love and have forgotten I exist, and I want to kill them for it.

Narcissism is a usefully mobile label for everything we want from other people, don't get, and never will. Possibly every couple-dispute at this stage in the evolution of modern subjectivity involves similar sorts of finger-pointing and reckonings. *"Do you think you're the only one who had a bad day?" "Do you ever think of anyone but yourself?"* To wit: how is the love pie being divided up and who's getting more of the good stuff? Who gets to be the center of the story and who's getting edged to the side at any given moment, with the prevalence of such disputes exacerbated by the fact that anyone sufficiently charismatic and complicated enough to hold your interest is inevitably going to be riddled with dangerous levels of narcissism, thus making the accusation moot while also a frequent point of friction?

If narcissism is the social character type in dominance, at least it's not our fault—it's postmodern life, the single-child family, the algorithms. Narcissism is the new herpes—it's not like you got it on purpose, you were just in the wrong place at the wrong time, then everyone's pointing fingers and trying to pretend they don't have it too.

—

Along with lethal spouses, another longtime popular entertainment staple: dating shows. Flipping between the two presents the amorous dialectic in a nutshell: either you're desperate to nab a mate and heartbroken they've chosen another contestant over you (as in *The Bachelor*'s brutal "elimination process," an important reminder that desirability is always a competition and you don't get the keys to the Fantasy Suite for being a nice person), or you're terrified that having nabbed them, they're now trying to do you in. I did become quite addicted to the pandemic's viral reality show hit *Indian Matchmaking,* a global capitalist update on the Jewish marriage broker joke, itself long one of my favorite genres. (My paternal grandparents had some bricklike compendium of Yiddish humor that I pored over as a child, hiding in the linen closet during family visits absorbed in the world of *shadchan* and *schnorrers* to tune out my grandparents' nonstop bickering.)

Sima Taparia, billed as Mumbai's top matchmaker, jets from place to place attempting to locate matches for her supremely picky clients, well-to-do Indians from New Delhi to New Jersey, who respond to her efforts with comments like "He wasn't everything on the checklist." You quickly realized that as much as everyone claims to be eager to enter the magic kingdom of coupledom, they're equally in flight from its demands and potential wounds, lonely but armed with checklists. A positive date was "I don't hate him. That's a big deal." (The show was criticized, including by Dalit writers, for normalizing caste discrimination and effacing colorism with innocuous phrases like "similar backgrounds.")

The theme really isn't tradition versus modernity or arranged marriages versus self-engineered ones (which are actually no more likely to "succeed," according to those who study these things), it's the universal desire to simultaneously couple and bolt. About her most picky client, Aparna, an Indian American lawyer in Houston, Sima diagnoses a "block in her energies" and sends her to an astrologist. The real problem is that Aparna, whose ambivalence is played for comic effect, is a great truth-teller—that is, in every respect Sima's worst nightmare. About the wedded state Aparna quips, "Oh, do we have to see our husbands all the time? Is that a thing people have to do? Because I'd rather not, I think." You may yearn for someone to wake up beside and fetch ginger ale when you have the flu, but the day-to-day reality is a flesh-and-blood other human being you have to contend with day in and out, whether you feel like it or don't, who comes equipped with a dumpster's worth of needs and "quirks," cracking unfunny jokes you're expected to laugh at and *wanting things from you.* Like to take you to a comedy club, as one potential date hideously suggests. Aparna hates comedy.

Freud was especially fond of marriage broker jokes, and

yes, they stink of misogyny and ableism to our enlightened ears—the potential brides invariably have flaws or
physical deformities that must be sold to hapless grooms as
advantages—but what better collected insights are there into
coupledom's enduring hang-ups? Early psychoanalysts took
such jokes as evidence that marriage itself was a neurotic
institution, and on that front they were a lot more honest
than the current breed. A frequent joke motif was the concept of the "ready-made," the idea that what looks at first
glance to be a dealbreaker will actually prove a blessing, or
so the matchmaker tries to convince potential grooms. "But
she has four children" cries a young man to the marriage broker who's trying to saddle him with the lady and the brood.
"My boy," replies the broker. "Did you ever stop to think that
if you married a maiden and decided to have four children,
what kind of *tsuris* you'd go through? Your apartment is
two flights up and you'd have to carry your wife up the stairs
when you bring her back from the hospital . . ." There follows
a lengthy spiel of woe involving sprained backs for him, rest
cures in the country for her, him stuck doing the diapers and
cooking . . . "Take the ready-made family!" urges the canny
broker.

A less comedic gloss was offered by Wilhelm Stekel, one
of Freud's original circle until a falling-out (Freud constantly
fell out with his acolytes, some think because he was homo-
erotically in love with them—everyone loves psychoanalyzing
Freud as if the idea that he too had an unconscious discredits

him rather than proving his brilliance). The two disagreed about masturbation, among other things—Stekel thought it was no big deal. Possibly he was a practitioner (rumors circulated). After the break the loyalists called him "morally insane," code for not falling in line.

In Stekel's version of the ready-made joke, a matchmaker tries to set up a rich girl with a young man, who points out that this isn't such a great offer given that the girl had once broken her leg and now limps. "What of it!" replies the matchmaker. "Just imagine that you were already married. You take your wife for a walk. Along comes an automobile and your wife is run down. You immediately call an ambulance, and you have to take your wife to the hospital. The doctor comes in. You go through a few weeks of the greatest excitement, then you have to come through for the big bills. But with her you have a finished product!"

Here we come to a disquieting conundrum: do we love our mates in spite of their wounds, or because of them? Stekel tells an anecdote to illustrate. A man runs into the wife of a friend of his on the street. She'd always left him cold but now he notices that she's bruised, and learns that her husband had beaten her up. He's suddenly overtaken by a wave of passion and practically falls on her. They go somewhere and have really great sex, both tremendously turned on for reasons they can't admit to themselves. The secret is that he's a sadist with too much conscience to act on his desires. For him, the friend's wife is a "finished product"—someone else hit her, not him. He's an innocent party! For her part, she wants revenge against her brutish husband, and sleeping with his friend is pretty gratifying payback. They're a perfect match, but for reasons that have nothing to do with who the other "really is," it's what they represent to each other, consciously or not, that bonds them. We make creative use of each other, in other words—*that's* the real thrill. In the best matches it's mutual—neurotic pacts don't work on a one-way basis.

Emotions always come trailing their opposite number, a central idea in the Freudian corpus that Stekel thought he didn't get sufficient credit for introducing. When he presented it as "mental bipolarity"—desire and disgust, love and hate, will to power and will to submission—the entire circle laughed and belittled him, but when his rival Eugen Bleuler, a Swiss eugenicist (big on sterilizing schizophrenics and the "mentally unfit," ideas that haven't aged well), rebranded it "ambivalence" in 1910 (combining the Latin *ambi,* meaning both, and *valentia,* meaning strength), they loved it and treated it like a shiny new toy. It's possible that Stekel's personality style irritated the loyalists—he doesn't seem to have lacked confidence.

And how much *is* hate bound up with love, or maybe even its prerequisite? I recall once visiting, in pre-COVID times, the home of an acquaintance whose partner, a brilliant philosopher, had been left twisted and hunchbacked by a childhood disease. I guiltily wondered whether my acquaintance managed to overlook the hunchback or was attracted to it.

Either way, she seemed my moral better, far more humane, or far more perverse. The partner was a bastard, insulting to everyone, especially my acquaintance. Was this too part of the attraction, or something she could overlook? (At his memorial service his son's eulogy included the line, "My dad didn't believe in bullshit so I'm not going to tell you what a wonderful guy he was.") I didn't understand the erotics of the relationship, but witnessing it felt like an indictment of my own conventionality. At one point I idly pulled a magazine down from a pile on a dusty end table—the place was in a state of squalor—and dislodged a stack of months-old unopened mail underneath. "How can people live like this?" I screamed silently inside my head, shamed by my bourgeois housekeeping standards but also really wanting to get home.

The thought I couldn't articulate at the time was Stekel's: Are there particular forms of woundedness we each search for in a beloved? That "work" for us? Let's not imagine the finished-product principle applies only to men in marriage broker jokes. Recall Jane Eyre (such a good little Christian!) and the imperious Mr. Rochester, who can get together as equals only after fate contrives to blind and maim him. Once humbled (once symbolically castrated), a "finished product"—with Jane, by another convenient twist of fate, suddenly rich—the two can settle into happy coupledom and love each other for eternity. He's the perfect repository for her unexpressed rage (and no doubt Brontë's, who had plenty of reasons to be rageful); she's spared from having to mutilate him herself, which would have made her an unsympathetic figure.

Is that what my beloved is to me, I sometimes wondered during our forced sequestration, did my buried animus toward men find expression in the wounds he's inflicted on himself (or were inflicted previously by the madwoman in the attic, his mother in this case)? Intimacy, subterranean motives, neurotic pact—all of the above? If you try to "fix" the neurotic portion, will attraction soon fizzle away? Nevertheless, fix we do, or valiantly attempt it. But how do you get the formula right: too much neurosis is toxic, too little is stultifying. A slight error in the recalibrating procedures could spell love's ruination.

As such questions indicate, the pandemic brought all sorts of "unhealthy dynamics" to light. Ours was a neurotic pact for sure, but at least it seemed a sustainable one. As lockdown dragged on and the world receded and we relied on each other for every last shred of emotional sustenance, I did become aware of previously untapped reservoirs of sadism bubbling up in me. I was mutating into a new, more diabolic version of myself. (The virologists call it "viral escape"—even viruses yearn to be something other than they are.) My boyfriend hates having the top of his head touched, which he likens to being treated like a dog, yet I was somehow unable to stop myself from *patting it* whenever we were watching TV and I got up to get something bad for me (wine, chocolate, chips) from the kitchen, which was frequently, and entailed passing behind his chair. Why I had this impulse I cannot say—a few strands of serial killer DNA lodged deep in a chromosome or two? The vulnerability of that noggin, the eternal, poignant masculine struggle between the invading forces of baldness and the Maginot Line of hair, brought out the worst in me. Eventually he just stopped complaining about it. I had successfully bent him to my will. I felt a new surge of intimacy flowing between us.

What a reservoir of oddity there must be at the core of every long-term couple, a fundamental queerness permeating the supposedly normal and normative. Stekel thought we shovel too many complex feelings into the paltry word, "love," and that it's unilluminating at best. How can one word encompass so many polarities? Having left an unhappy first marriage himself ("You marry a woman you love to find next morning that you have married a stranger"), he's nothing if not eloquent on the constraints of coupledom. "I once ventured to define marriage as the condition in which the slaver of the one party is tempered by the non-freedom of the other," he wrote in 1930. Everyone enters matrimony mourning their lost freedom in other words, though endlessly trying to prove you're free quickly turns into its own sort of prison too.

If you're anything like me, you pray to the gods of coupled intimacy to spare you such conflicts, though they're obviously inbuilt. You're grateful someone's willing to put up with you and resentful of the demands they put on your time; happy to have someone nearby to have sex with when you feel like it and bitter about renouncing other possibilities (even where such possibilities are nonexistent); comforted by the partner's "thereness" and stifled by the manufactured jealousies and weird fixations. You'd think being housebound would alleviate jealousy problems but think again; our capacity for triangulation is infinite—perhaps a crafty way of keeping desire's flame flickering. Someone in my circle "accidentally noticed" on her partner's open laptop a work email to one of his colleagues who happens to be both well-known and rather hot. Somehow it seemed like a good idea to email the famous hot colleague and explain that her partner had once had an "emotional affair" via email with a previous colleague, and she wasn't comfortable with the two of them corresponding. In no world was this a good idea, but by that point every marriage had become its own unique failed state, mirroring geopolitical conditions worldwide. Our borders felt vulnerable, and vulnerability demands more intensive policing. They split up soon after, another pandemic casualty.

Everyone has a secret demand in love that can't be met; we live under regimes of perpetual renunciation. However illusory what's being renounced may be—your freedom? what freedom?—renunciation is still required, and life without illusions can be tedious and gray. "Both parties bleed from no fault of their own," diagnosed Stekel, who ditched one wife for another he felt better understood by. Maybe it's the things we're most split about that hold us tightest in their grip.

Recently I asked a shrink I know if she'd noticed any themes among her patients during COVID times. She said everyone had a fantasy that other people were doing better. The singles envied the couples, the couples envied the singles, the people with kids envied the people without kids, and so on. All her patients had regressed in different ways, which I entirely understood (meaning "entirely identified with"). Between COVID lockdown and the flailing government response it was like being locked in your bedroom with a sibling while a crazy abusive parent rants in the living room making shit up and changing the story. Everyone felt deprived of something essential, said my shrink friend. There was so much loneliness, no less among the coupled. I suppose I'd asked because I was looking for glimpses into how people were living and loving in such uncertain times, and how they projected themselves into the future. I guess I was asking how I could continue to live and love with so much uncertainty. How do you stay in love with the world amid so much loss? Nevertheless, you love, you're injured and inflict injuries, you throw people away then try to get them back, we yearn for one another in sickness and in health.

2

VILE BODIES: HETEROSEXUALITY AND ITS DISCONTENTS

To burglarize Marx, we don't make love under circumstances we choose, we make love under the circumstances we inherit, and even pre-pandemic, the inherited circumstances had been feeling pretty toxic when it came to bodily matters. And that was before quite as many bodies were literally contagious. If love is a matter of attractions and repulsions, of bodies and how they collide, the afflictions of the social body bleed into our individual desires and disgusts too. Consider the recent maladies in the sphere of heterosexuality, as a significant portion of the world's population does still align with this creed and conducts their love lives accordingly, and there isn't enough hand sanitizer in the world to scrub the taint off this enterprise.

Just as the death rate from COVID in the U.S. unmasked the enduring inequalities of the American political system, #MeToo exposed that heterosexuality as traditionally practiced had long been on a collision course with the imperatives of gender parity. The aftermath has been, for many, decidedly rocky. For legions of women worldwide, men had started feeling like germs, though germs you didn't mind occasionally getting horizontal with. Legions of men spent sleepless nights wondering which disgruntled former girlfriend or drunken hook-up would be tweeting their crimes or calling their bosses. In my own household certain formerly tolerated behaviors began to be tagged with labels like "privileged" and "typical." Then New York governor Andrew Cuomo, previously a COVID hero and the object of many straight women's lust ("Cuomosexuals"), was brought down in a #MeToo fusillade, accused of the same kind of workplace sexual harassment he'd signed legislation to help prevent. He claimed in his resignation speech that he'd only been practicing old school charm as he understood it: "In my mind, I've never crossed the line with anyone, but I didn't realize the extent to which the line has been redrawn."

My point is that personal life isn't just personal. For any of us. We're infected by history no less than by viruses, by those we hate no less than those we love. And a lot of hatreds have been unleashed in the last few years.

To recap: At the beginning, it was a bunch of reprehensible media potentates crashing to earth, soon followed by a collection of lesser despots and lords, many employed in the media industries too. That quickly expanded to include half the men in Hollywood and ancillary trades like politics. It turned out that famous pundits had been rubbing their pants-encased erections against underlings and job applicants, powerful movie producers were masturbating into potted plants, legendary editors sticking their tongues in their employees' mouths as if mining for gold, hairy hands everywhere. Men previously lauded for intellectual seriousness had been greeting their assistants garbed in open bathrobes, everything dangling; brazen demands for sexual servicing long the norm among guys who thought the world owed them b.j.s on demand.

The stories that emerged were grotesque, each more scummy than the last. In the tallest skyscrapers and plushest hotels of the most advanced economies, significant numbers of high-profile men had been acting the part of feudal lords, demanding *droit du seigneur* from their vassals, the vassals in this case being their female employees and others wishing entry into their fiefdoms. Evidently there'd been a covert system of taxation on female advancement in the work world, with the unluckier among us obligated to render not just the usual fealty demanded by overweening bosses but varying degrees of sexual homage too, from ego-stroking and fluffing (which is gross enough), to being grabbed and groped, to the expectation of silence about full-on rape.

Not unfamiliar stuff to anyone who'd been paying attention for the last hundred or so years, since the advent of Hollywood and women entering the workforce, but suddenly the media was all over it: the violated were going on the record recounting their experiences of violation, and the honchos were falling, splat splat. An international plague of shitty men was being exposed and dethroned; *The New York Times* started keeping a running photo array of disgraced bigwigs, updated daily like heads on pikes after the storming of the Bastille. All we were talking about that year were the fallen men—every day another wrecked career, sometimes two or three. The air felt thick with sexual antipathy and grievance. Was male hegemony finally in the toilet? "Time's up!" you everywhere heard, which was exciting, though in certain ways also confusing.

The confusing part was the way that male sexuality itself—often invasive, yet for at least some percentage of self-identified heterosexual women also a turn-on—had been fast reconfigured as a moral hazard and psychological threat, a social disease we needed protection from. Once diagnosed by Adrienne Rich as a political institution not a desire, heterosexuality became, with #MeToo, an international crime scene, an infringement of human rights whose traumatic effects women suffered disproportionately. Men had had impunity to be sexually disgusting for way too long (millennia). Look at them swaggering around—the world needed a vaccine against them, and #MeToo was that vaccine. The long-term efficacy remains unknown, but with legacy media, the internet, higher ed and H.R. offices nationwide all joining forces with fed-up women to declare an institutional reckoning on male sexual privilege, that's a pretty powerful set of alliances. There were new sheriffs in town and the one-strike rule was in effect. Heads would keep rolling, including for decades-old offenses when previous behavioral tenets had been in effect, but it wasn't the moment to quibble about niceties.

At first the battleground was careers and the enemies being slain the career gatekeepers. A struggle over careers is, to be sure, a bourgeois revolution (I mean this in the historical not the disparaging sense), in the tradition of previous democratic revolutions fought over self-sovereignty and citizenship. Or that's how I saw it—I was exhilarated and wrote that we were in the midst of a radical uprising, and that if women's bodies were still being treated as feudal property at this late date then another Reign of Terror was long overdue, and this social stratum needed to be liquidated before all the genders could achieve civic and economic equality. I believe I cited Gramsci.

But the picture kept changing, the enemies list expanding. Soon a lot of not-very-powerful men were under fire too—freelance writers and experimental novelists (nobody's bosses but their own) were on the hit list, and the accusations could be pretty vague. Writers of color were getting picked off, maybe disproportionately. We were running out of potentates. The supply of moral monsters was dwindling, so new ogres had to be located to keep the momentum up. Someone I used to have lunch with occasionally was called out for "weird lunch 'dates'" on an anonymous crowdsourced online spreadsheet of shitty men in media, and I tried to interpret what the scare quotes around "dates" meant. Had our lunches been weird and I hadn't realized it? Was he weird with other women and not with me—didn't I rate? A few friends confessed they'd never been harassed and wondered if there was something wrong with them, but this was always said *sotto voce*—people would literally look around to make sure no one was listening. You had to know someone pretty well to get jocular on this subject.

The rest of us were checking ourselves for bruises, combing our pasts for perpetrators, dredging up bad memories however trifling and posting them online (I heard this referred to as the "Weinstein effect"). What had previously been an "uncomfortable encounter" now had yellow police tape around it. Generational chasms were cracking open, with younger (millennial, Gen Z) women on the warpath about the kinds of experiences older (boomer, Gen X) women had been accustomed to shrugging off as no big deal, and much muttering on each side about the cluelessness or anti-feminism, or ageism or excess fragility, of the other cohort.

Speaking of disease vectors, I've sometimes wondered if #MeToo would have had the success it did absent the lingering post-HIV consciousness of sex as potentially fatal. It's difficult to recall, even for those who were actually sentient pre-AIDS, that brief interregnum between the headiness of the sexual revolution and that dark day in 1983 when the HIV-1 virus was first isolated, back when sex seemed imbued with *healthful* properties—really, it was regarded as almost a balm. STDs notwithstanding, it cured people of things—uptightness, for instance. There were rumors it was "liberating," at least according to progressives. It could end wars, if you believed the counterculture. Even when it was bad, as it often was, it wasn't really bad *for* you, just disappointing, like a subpar restaurant meal. As the HIV crisis unfolded, gay activists were putting out brave pamphlets with titles like "How to Have Sex During an Epidemic," trying not to die while also saving sexual liberation from moral opportunists and do-gooders.

Feminists, by contrast, have been in contention about sex since day one—*pleasure* or *danger,* to reference a landmark 1980s anthology—with the danger crowd effectively stomping the competition. (Congrats to them, they had better strategies.) I'm not saying that one version of the story is truer than the other: it's ideology all the way down. The stories we tell about what sex means ebb and shift in the cultural winds and never for one reason alone, but how a population talks about sex ("sexual discourse") conditions how a population *feels* about sex, and no doubt what it feels like to actually *have* sex. We're a suggestible species and viruses aren't the only contagions around—so are ideas and feelings. Culture works by transmission.

Cut to now. If it's possible to describe "what's in the air"—what you inhale from the cultural mulch, the thrum of strangers feeling and existing, their overheard conversations, the pong of collective anxiety—my "sense of things" is that the mood is not exactly joyous lately when it comes to the male-female thing. Because listen, I feel this shift in myself. I'm suggestible too. You can turn your head or hold your nose but you're still inhaling the cultural winds.

To quote the sexual reprobate Michel Houellebecq, "I'm simplifying here but sometimes you have to simplify or you end up with nothing." To put it simply, the sociosexual situation just feels a lot ickier than it used to. Encountering sex unexpectedly, like when it leaps out from the wrong source—even when it's just a glance or a joke, or god forbid (in pre-pandemic days) a touch . . . I know *intellectually* that there's not *more* sexual assault or predation than there used to be—I hasten to add that of course *any* is too much—and that by most measures sexual violence has in fact dropped in the U.S., along with violent crime generally ever since the 1990s. Yet something just makes sex feel grosser and more dangerous, even if you fought on the "pleasure" side in the Great Feminist Wars of the last few decades.

Gay men may have been the demographic more associated with HIV in this part of the world, but somehow it was heterosexual sex that came to *seem* riskier and more treacherous in the post-AIDS decades, at least compared to the bustling sexual carnival of the before-HIV years. If not to your physical health, then to your emotional well-being. Especially if the "you" in question is female. According to the new cultural givens, sexual predators roam the planet inflicting damage and exploitation. Intergenerational desire is now especially to be feared, providing a new class of cultural villain, since current lore dictates that such desires can never be reciprocal. Because "grooming" (a term once reserved for pedophiles approaching children, now deployed when there's an age difference greater than five years between two parties if the younger person is female and under twenty-five, according to my visibly disgusted students discussing the dating habits of certain male celebrities). There's much talk about the trauma of bad sexual experiences, the effects of which can last for life, embedded in your deepest recesses, as ineradicable as HIV had once been.*

The question one brings up at one's peril is where the new lines should be drawn. It's not sexuality alone that's become problematic, anything merely "sex-adjacent" has been transformed into a pollutant, including jokes, those teensy unregulated libidinal outstations. The failed joke has always been a sad little specimen, but the quip that would formerly have gotten a polite half-laugh or eyeroll is now a dangerous toxin,

---

* The impact of #MeToo on gay male culture is a story for someone else to write, but the heightened horror about intergenerational sex and the premise that it can only cause deep harm has made inroads even in these milieus, I'm told, particularly for millennial queers.

not to mention a window onto the male unconscious, where bad jokes originate and ferment until they stink like bovine farts, polluting the gender ecosystem.

The cultural sanitation project is still going strong, with loss of livelihood the penalty for misfired witticisms, even when they misfire on a private Facebook page. As happened to one of my Facebook friends, formerly a well-regarded National Public Radio movie critic who, when director Bernardo Bertolucci died in 2018, posted (then quickly deleted) a quip about the notorious anal rape scene in *Last Tango in Paris*. "Even grief is better with butter," he wrote (butter featured in the staged scene), accompanied by a still of Maria Schneider and Marlon Brando. You can hear him straining and failing to find the clever take, a condition that afflicts anyone who spends too much time on social media and gets addicted to those endorphin-boosting "likes." Sadly for him, one of his 2,000 or so "friends" (not me) screenshotted the post and passed it on to a feminist actress and sometimes radio host who tweeted it to *her* 196,000 followers along with the demand: "Fire him. Immediately." Which happened the next day. (A mid-tier actress getting to bring down a powerful film critic—what sweeter vindication is there?) Note that at the time of its release *Last Tango* was regarded as an edgy masterpiece. These are, as mentioned, different times.

No doubt many regard the evolution of gendered management styles from "Give me a blow job or I'll fire you" to "Don't tell a joke I don't like or I'll fire you" as a social advance. We've long heard that the solution to the world's problems is putting more women in positions of power and that when that finally happens the world will be a more humane place, because women's style of rule will be different from men's. More peaceable, fairer and more collaborative— a more *moral* style of power than the masculinist versions we've been forever subjected to. Regarding the cultural clean-up squads, one hears occasional grumbling (mostly from libertarians and the right) about due process and "trial by internet," but unless you want to be lambasted as a rape apologist and tarred with being on "the wrong side of history" you're advised to pick your occasions on this score.

Given all this gleeful cultural policing—or "feminism with blood on its hands," in the words of Janet Halley, a feminist law professor at Harvard with no love of feminism's carceral turn—I have some questions, as they say online. For instance: are we just installing a new breed of autocrat in place of the old autocrats? Yes, fire on-the-job gropers and harassers, fire them hard. But is the treatment of the workforce more humane when there's no "off the clock"? If it's company time all the time? There's been astoundingly little pushback about the vast expansion of employers' power over workers' leisure hours. Are workers' rights one of those vanishing "privileges" we're just supposed to adapt to?

The political problem of women's liberation for a leftist-feminist is that the "liberation" part was long ago left by the wayside. Who needs emancipation—abortion rights, free maternity and childcare would have been places to start—when there are unfunny jokesters to punish? "Emancipation" isn't a term you hear much these days in feminist contexts, it's not exactly where the cultural energy is. The seductions of authoritarianism have won the day. But if we're weeding out vestigial patriarchal elements and replacing them with new values, overturning millennia of oppressive male power one film critic at a time, shouldn't the purge criteria at least be made explicit? Do dumb jokes cause such irreparable harm that firing is the only remedy? Are jokes an x-ray of the soul and clear souls now required to remain employed? Are jokes to be taken entirely literally, rather than occasionally meaning their opposite (as a Freudian might insist), which is obviously creatively stifling, but who cares because creative freedom is a dangerous liberal cultural value? If these are the new rules, what's being demanded is a pretty *large-scale* cultural and psychological overhaul. Like of the entirety of mental life.

About #MeToo and its aftermath, I became of many minds. Asked to write a commentary on an anti-#BalanceTonPorc open letter (or "OutYourPigs"—the French version of the movement) signed by Catherine Deneuve and a hundred other French women, I too dutifully dredged up a memory from decades ago, not a particularly traumatizing one, just the usual indignity of life in a female body. The Deneuve letter had bemoaned that men were being asked to give up the "right to bother," which seemed to be enumerating an all-*new* right for men. This seemed willfully perverse—don't they have enough of them already? Don't they exercise them *all the time*?

The memory was of heading into a restaurant with a group of people when a man I barely knew who was walking behind me, a British journalist friend of a friend—someone later to become politically illustrious as a Labor MP and Europe minister—reached forward and grabbed my ass. I'm being overly delicate—not just grabbed, he stuck his fingers *in* my ass; in other words, he goosed me. It was humiliating and incensing but I was young and didn't know what to do, so I just turned around and glared at him, then kept walking. Whereupon he did it again. I think he smirked. The thing is that unlike most such stories this one actually turned out well. What I mean is that he later went to prison. The ostensible reason was for extravagantly cheating on his expenses, but I prefer to think it was cosmic justice for his crimes against my person. Here was someone perfectly willing to take what wasn't his due in any sphere and I was more than delighted to see him put away, if only for a brief six weeks.*

It intrigued me to encounter this gloating, punitive streak in my psyche—it's not like I don't get, at very deep levels, the

---

* Like Eldridge Cleaver and Dreyfus, he wrote a prison memoir upon his release.

allures of carceral feminism. At the same time, I understand what's at stake for the women who'd signed the awkward *lettre française*. The shared anxiety is that the new regulatory spirit encroaches on zones and behaviors we might call "sexually liminal": innuendos, come-ons, banter, "stolen kisses." For many women, especially of the heterosexual persuasion, these in-between zones are what makes life worth living. Flirting is where your desirability is confirmed; men stealing kisses opens up new possibilities; something unexpected and maybe thrilling has occurred. Male sexual license can be hot—it's long been thought, and the French in particular like to think so, that crossing boundaries is what makes sex exciting and literary. (Note that this is a precept increasingly under reexamination even in France, as once-celebrated boundary-crossers are being threatened with hoosegowing, and their victims now the ones writing the best sellers.)

The larger part of me says yeah, bring the clueless fuckers down, let heads roll. I loved seeing all those smug and powerful guys toppled, though once on their knees, they often seemed pretty pathetic. The accepted wisdom is that sexual harassment isn't about sex it's about power, though I sometimes wonder if that underthinks the situation. About those chopped-down potentates and lords: many, one couldn't help noticing, were not the most attractive specimens on the block. Bulbous, jowly men; fat men who told women they needed to lose weight; ugly men drawn to industries organized around female appearance. Men with weird hair. Is it wrong of me to bring this up? Is the man who won't stop talking about sex and hitting on his underlings someone convinced of his power, or a threatened runt? You can say it's immaterial, but if recent events have told us anything it's that power is a social agreement, not some sort of stable entity. Which we forget at peril of our complicity with it.

Conversations with friends inevitably turned, in those early festal #MeToo days, often with dark hilarity, to the physical hideousness of so many of the accused men. Sometimes the levity was tinged with guilt—having been subject to the brutality of appearance rankings our entire lives, shouldn't we refrain from imposing them on others? Still, surveying the photo arrays of the perps, you suspected that these were mostly not the sought-after guys in high school. Now, old and smug, bloated with power and fine cuisine, their physical unloveliness gave the unfolding story a pleasing Grimm-like quality: they'd acted monstrously, and they looked the part.

The fact is that we move through the world as embodied creatures, for better or worse. I wondered what it felt like, if you're such a guy, someone who'd managed to accrue some significant portion of power in the world, but you're still *you* (who ever really gets past high school?), coercing sex out of underlings. When you look in the mirror, is it a great white hunter you see staring back, with women your game of choice, or a pimply loser? Sure you've *won,* you're on *top,* you've got that mantel of Oscars and Emmys, but isn't every strong-armed conquest just a jab of confirmation about your a priori loathsomeness? A model who'd had to lock herself in a bathroom to escape a naked Harvey Weinstein's advances recalled that he'd "whimpered" and accused her of rejecting him because he was fat.

When the unindicted war criminal Henry Kissinger, known as an espouser of *"Realpolitik,"* famously said back in the last century that power is the ultimate aphrodisiac (for many decades regarded as a sophisticated truism), what he actually meant, I think, is that given social conditions in which power is unequally distributed according to gender, power makes unattractive men more alluring. Attractive men don't need aphrodisiacs, physical attractiveness is its own aphrodisiac. The Kissinger fantasy was that power "sweeps a girl off her feet" in the way that charisma does, or how it works for rock stars. Were the harassers rock stars in their own imaginations? "He's a rock star," people now say fawningly about every C.E.O. with a good fourth quarter, and obviously plenty of them started to believe it, misrecognizing every woman in the vicinity as a compliant groupie.

Male power may have a sleazier connotation lately than in Kissinger's heyday, the gender imbalances may be slowly getting less unbalanced, but the truism isn't obsolete: power is still a fungible currency and sufficient quantities of it offset shortfalls in physical appeal. If in doubt, take a look at the society page photos of rich old men and their trophy wives, or Hollywood producers and their arm candy, or Donald Trump and Melania. Each party brings their assets to market and strikes the best bargain they can, that's sexual *Realpolitik*. (It was never clear if Kissinger thought the arrangement works the same way for powerful women, though one suspects not.)

If power is an aphrodisiac that lets unsightly men nab beautiful women, among the problems for the nabbed is that it's not a symmetrical arrangement: whatever power beauty confers on women is precarious—the sell-by date, the replaceability. Those eighty-plus allegations against the sexual Godzilla Harvey Weinstein were an archive of information about such realities, exposing some pretty harsh social truths. It was one story after another about women navigating Hollywood offices and hotel rooms in a system weighted toward sexual exploitation, where looks and sexual allure have always been the entrance ticket for career advancement. And extracting sexual kowtowing from women has always been, for some men, a perquisite of power. In a system already rigged for sexual manipulation, what was most notable about Harvey Weinstein was that he tried to rig it even more, with such relentlessness and regularity it was almost like he was on autopilot.

As friends shared accounts of harassment and gross come-ons in the early #MeToo months, I noticed an interesting theme emerging, something I hadn't previously considered. Being hit on by someone you judged unattractive was regarded as more insulting than being encroached on by someone decent-looking. A friend who'd once had to physically fight off a drunken but not uncomely movie star with whom she'd shared a limo described the ordeal with amused annoyance, but a mild overture from an aging, balding editor who looked like a potato in horn-rims (her description) left her fuming. It was a sudden glimpse into a complicated set of internal sociosexual calculations that (I suspect) most of us perform unconsciously all the time. Clearly it's the harassing behavior itself that's objectionable, but being harassed by someone you regard as in a different attractiveness echelon compounds the affront. Perhaps it risks lowering you in your own esteem—does he think he's in my league?

Everyone knows the principle of "assortative mating," even those who aren't familiar with the phrase. It refers to our tendency to pick mates who are similar to ourselves in characteristics like class and education, and also, of course, physical attractiveness. I'm saying nothing a customer of Tinder or Hinge would find surprising—the more attractive you are the more attractive you want your mate to be, other things being equal. But other things aren't always equal: power and money allow people (primarily male people) to jump the queue. And if the #MeToo moment puts this pretty entrenched dynamic up for reconsideration, that *would* be a truly radical overhaul of the body politic, and all our "personal" lives.

There's no doubt that loving someone can make them attractive regardless of physiognomy, that you can be sexually attracted to people you don't necessarily find physically beautiful, and every permutation on the theme, but the extra purchasing power men have traditionally wielded in the heterosexual marketplace is among the things currently being renegotiated. When I decided to crowdsource the attractiveness question online, my women friends were eager to weigh in. "I think it's important for female humans to express their distaste for such male bodies," said one. "Men like these have long lived with the assumption their flesh is tolerable, and some may believe it's desirable." They were by turns biting and gleeful on the subject—I sensed that deriding men's looks felt to them like taking a political stand; letting men experience the same kind of vulnerability women endure seemed like a small victory. These victories could be exceedingly small—recall that Melania Trump was often (improbably) regarded on feminist Twitter as some kind of stealth ally for appearing to visibly recoil when her husband tried to hold her hand, despite also being a leading international spokesmodel for sexual barter and its reward structures.

The fact is that women finding men disgusting is a modern achievement. As literary scholar Ruth Perry outlines in her wryly titled essay "Sleeping with Mr. Collins," female sexual disgust was little evident prior to the eighteenth century, and even as late as Jane Austen's *Pride and Prejudice* (1813), when Charlotte Lucas marries the repellent Mr. Collins in a "pragmatic match" and talks things over post-nuptials with her girlfriends, there's no hint that having sex or sharing a bed with an odious man was repellent. Perry's point is that sex didn't have the same psychological resonance as it does for the contemporary psyche. To the modern sensibility, marriage to a man you find repellent is a version of prostitution; in former times it was routine. Perry herself clearly feels so much physical repugnance at the idea of sleeping with Mr. Collins she's practically shuddering on the page.

As the nineteenth century unfolded and companionate marriages became the norm, with romantic sentiments rather than their kinfolk's aspirations dictating women's marital choices, our somatized reactions to the male body were likewise transformed. For Perry, the rise of sexual disgust meant that female sexuality henceforth wasn't just a component of physical life, it was getting psychologized, becoming part of who we *are* at the deepest levels. As the nineteenth-century novel so assiduously cataloged, with its keen eye for the dissatisfaction married heroines experienced toward husbands formerly procured for pragmatic reasons, and female novel readers invited to share their repugnance. What more plodding blunderer than Charles Bovary? Who'd want to bed him—except that when "good husband material" was based on pounds per annum and there weren't other options if you, like Emma, wanted to get off the farm, sexual disgust wasn't an affordable luxury.

In other words, heightened levels of sexual delicacy didn't just spring from within our deepest beings, it was tied to material considerations. Which makes me wonder how much women's increasing financial independence, including the option to live life without a man or choose queerness in any of its flavors, has contributed to men seeming so much more encroaching and disgusting these days, including their jokes and mild overtures?

To put the question in more sweeping terms, can heterosexuality survive gender parity?

Note that being a successful sexual pragmatist at present requires the ability to adopt a pre-modern obliviousness about sexual disgust—too much sensitivity would impede effective bartering. Those choosing to sleep with the Mr. Collinses of our time have it far rougher than Charlotte Lucas did. Occasionally those calculations and their inner toll bursts into view—cf. TMZ and Page Six on the sometimes-vicious divorce proceedings of aging male celebs and tycoons, with their former wives and lady pals dishing about sagging flesh and flagging sex lives. I too shared the cultural fascination with Melania Trump—bought and paid for by a repellent man toward whom she occasionally showily displayed her disgust, as if that annulled the arrangement, flaunting an autonomy she didn't possess to the world as if we'd all admire her for it. The Weinstein trial showcased the same tension, with accusers venting about how physically disgusting they'd found him despite, in some cases, participating in consensual sexual arrangements that continued for years and included declarations of love (even after previous episodes of rape and sexual assault). A startling moment came when one accuser testified that Weinstein appeared to be intersex (this made international headlines) and seemed deformed down there: he had no testicles, had mysterious scarring or burns in the genital region, and took shots to get erections. Also he smelled like shit.

Over his lawyers' objections, and for no discernible evidentiary purpose, the prosecution was permitted to display photos of Weinstein's naked body to the jury. Weinstein wasn't disputing that his accusers had seen his body, the dispute was over whether they'd consented to sex, about which naked photos wouldn't be dispositive. Presumably the motive for introducing them was establishing that Weinstein was so generally repellent no one would bed him voluntarily. It was baffling that they were legally admissible, but then again they were definitely in tune with the requirements of the cultural moment: men are basically deformed.*

The Weinstein photos also brought to mind the day, a few months before the 2016 election, when a half-dozen six-foot-five effigies of a naked Donald Trump, then the Republican presidential nominee—bulging paunch, saggy ass, constipated visage, shriveled micropenis—popped up simultaneously in

---

* Journalist Phoebe Eaton reported in *Airmail* later that year that Weinstein had contracted a life-threatening bacterial infection of the genital region known as Fournier's gangrene in 1999. Diabetics and middle-aged men are most vulnerable to it and skin grafts can be required to repair the area—extreme cases require an orchiectomy, meaning removal of the testicles. (I have no idea if this is true.)

cities around the country. Reading about them, I'd briefly liked being an American. We were tragic absurdists, a nation of disgusted pranksters. The statues, fabricated by an anarchist collective, had no balls. Like most women, I've never been entirely clear on what balls are for or why they're meant to symbolize traits like courage and daring. Aren't they actually the most vulnerable spot on a man—is that how men conquered the world, by costuming their vulnerabilities as mettle? (Something I wish I were better capable of, for the record.)

If disgust with male bodies is to be an effective idiom for disgust with malevolently racist and kleptocratic political institutions, obviously it helps if the male bodies in the news are objectively disgusting. At some level, you sort of knew that bodily aesthetics shouldn't bear the burden of moral judgments and political animus, but let's face it, political disgust and bodily disgust have long enjoyed a robust partnership, in fact, caricature was invented to turn the powerful into grotesques. (Lucky us, we got four years of a president permanently set to auto-caricature.)

It's said we choose leaders who make themselves legible to us as a collective mirror, that a leader's body signifies the dilemmas of the nation. Why else do you find yourself dreaming about them—exactly because you can't censor your dreams. History seeps in there too. Leaders become leaders by acting, consciously or unconsciously, in ways that make them seem clothed in metaphor. Maybe to an even greater degree than non-sociopathic leaders past and present, Trump was our man. He inspired #MeToo. How he brandished his body is our story too. Trump left one of my Facebook friends, a journalist, smeared with semen after he (allegedly) assaulted her in a Bergdorf Goodman dressing room twenty-five years ago. I've never met her, but even at this safe remove I too feel polluted, permanently smeared with the man. No one's immune.

There was a weird resonance between the exposure of Weinstein's nether regions and those naked Donald Trump effigies, titled, as it happens, "The Emperor Has No Balls." Something about disgust with male power and men's bodies is being renegotiated in public lately, if in messy inconclusive ways. They're being denuded and humiliated, the veils lifted to expose that something that was supposed to be there isn't. And what's the implication—that male power is done? That—as Gramsci would have it—consent to the previous hierarchies is being retracted? That patriarchy was a bluff all along?

Well . . . not so fast. The summer after #MeToo broke I noticed a thing going around the internet about "Big Dick Energy," which had started when someone tweeted that Anthony Bourdain, the celebrity chef and author who'd recently killed himself, had had it; then the singer Ariana Grande tweeted that her then-boyfriend, the comedian Pete Davidson, had a ten-inch dick and people started saying that he had it too. Suddenly a discussion was raging online about whether BDE, as it was soon known, required actually possessing a humongous physical organ or was more like a kind of *aura* or *inner life force,* and listicles started springing up about which male celebrities had it and which ones didn't. Given the faux-progressive spirit in these venues, it was soon agreed that women too could have BDE—Beyoncé definitely had it, also Serena Williams and Cate Blanchett; conversely a guy could have a colossal dick but lack BDE or even convey its opposite, "Little Dick Energy," because BDE was all about *inner* confidence, not an anatomical thing swinging between your legs. It was about *humility,* and not trying too hard or caring how you look, actually it was the complete opposite of "cockiness" as traditionally understood. Though having an actual big dick wasn't exactly bad, in fact there was something hot about it. Emblematic of "Little Dick Energy" was (no surprise) Donald Trump, joined by a parade of male celebs whose vibe didn't align with the sensibilities of the moment. (Justin Bieber, yes; Justin Timberlake, no.)

Big Dick Energy later made the Oxford English Dictionary shortlist for "Word of the Year." The winner—the single word or phrase that best captured the "ethos, mood, or preoccupations" of 2018—was "toxic." I suppose the scrambled dialectic between the two contenders is what I'm trying to get at. Was BDE an Owl of Minerva thing—were we celebrating it because somewhere deep in the collective unconscious it was end times for patriarchy, and the phallus was losing its symbolic currency? "The owl of Minerva spreads its wings only with the coming of the dusk," said Hegel, meaning we recognize the pinnacle of something only at the moment of its impending dissolution. We philosophize about things that are on their way out the door.

Or was BDE a revanchist move—was there still a residual fondness for big dicks, or big phalluses, or whatever amalgam was under discussion here; still some life in the old paradigm yet? Critics of BDE wanted to know why reducing men's worth to their bodies was any more acceptable than reducing women's worth to their bodies, and wasn't this just reinforcing the same gender binary we were supposed to be dismantling? Followers of the French psychoanalyst Jacques Lacan (Lacanian feminism was once a big thing in academic precincts) had produced ten thousand journal articles explicating the distinction between a phallus and a penis—one was symbolic and the other anatomical—and the important consequences of the distinction for humankind, though Lacan himself apparently sometimes slipped and referred to a penis as a "real" phallus.

In the BDE update, big dicks have phallic power that natal women too can share, to add to the fun. Nevertheless, even *if* the phallus is illusory, when the symbolics of power or coolness remain propped up by anatomical maleness, don't men (and those with male identities, regardless of anatomy—let's throw trans men in there too) remain the beneficiaries? In not uncontested ways, naturally. Mid-pandemic, the rapper Cardi B joined with Megan Thee Stallion to release "WAP" (an acronym for "Wet-Ass Pussy") to much acclaim; it was

widely seen as an anthem of female empowerment for center-
ing vagina braggadocio where rap had traditionally centered
dick braggadocio.

More than ever (or even more than usual), it was seeming as though the segment of the female population sexually
attracted to men was in a conflicted position. Throughout the
Western world, women were toiling to bring men down, yet
a rather significant number also still desired them for sex and
romantic purposes, which was producing no small amount
of neurotic self-contradiction. If heterosexuality is increasingly ethically suspect and morally contaminated, what are
conditions like in the dating trenches these days? Can we have
heterosexuality without heteronormativity? What does heterosexual desire feel like as gender equity gets tantalizingly
closer to being a reality?

So far the answer is "painfully confused." A recent letter to
a *Slate* sex advice columnist—"I'm a Heterosexual Woman
Who's Politically Opposed to Heterosexuality. Who Do I
Date?"—described the dilemma with both admirable preci-
sion and intensive murkiness. "I'm a cis woman in kind of
a classic millennial sex pickle: I'm really repelled by heterosexuality politically and personally, but I'm also really into
dick. I've been thinking maybe I should look for bi dudes/
bicurious gay dudes, but I am not sure how best to do that.
Rich, what would you think of a woman being on Grindr or

Scruff?" (These are gay male dating apps.) The writer wanted to be respectful of gay men's spaces, but also find a vers guy (men who don't have a position preference when they have sex with other men; willing to penetrate or be penetrated) who was open to dating women. She signed herself "Radical." The (gay male) advice columnist reminded her that there are plenty of shitty men who identify as gay and bi, and queerness doesn't automatically absolve anyone of misogyny, adding that "at least straight guys will pretend to be civilized for the sake of getting laid." (He also mildly derided her flavor of "self-flagellating dick politics.")

This is where we are at the moment.

If blowing up the old categories and binaries was supposed to be liberatory, liberation is proving elusive. Right-wing pundits love to dismiss this kind of thing as campus leftism, though for the actual (anti-capitalist) left it's the dead end of liberal identity politics. As debates rage about what to call it and who's responsible for it, sex itself appears to be getting infinitely more miserable. Young people are still having it occasionally, though vastly less this century than their predecessors last century, and college students are having least of all, say the people who collect statistics on this stuff. The social concern-mongers are happy to wag their well-meaning fingers at porn, and there's no doubt that sexual fashion lately leans toward the porny and baroque: anal is the new second base. (An AIDS activist I know refers to this as the homosexualization of straight sex—all the conversation about anal sex and how to do it safely in the HIV era got straight people curious about it, he believes.) There's also a lot of choking going on—40 percent of the under-thirty cohort say they've choked someone or been choked, not always consensually. If it were possible to turn sex into something very unpleasant, it appears that's the plan—hearing that college students are having infrequent sex and fleeing the gender binary, it's not hard to understand why. Importantly, the increases in sexual sophistication have yet to be matched by increases in female agency. You come across painful letters to sex advice columnists from young women not sure how to tell their male sex partners, especially on a first date, that they don't wish to be strangled.

Rough sex is big these days, some percentage of it not entirely consensual, a contributing factor in the explosion of campus assault charges too. A leading Title IX lawyer says that probably half the student cases he gets involve rough sex gone wrong. The off-campus justice system—online exposés and Twitter takedowns of perps—features much the same stories. In one saga I followed, four different women, all young writers or working in media, turned out to have had physically abusive relationships with the same guy, a Brooklyn-based freelance writer they'd all first met on Twitter or Tinder. They discovered their interconnection only when one of them, Helen—prompted by the revelations about Harvey Weinstein—tweeted photos of her bruised face and body from when she'd dated him. Whereupon the others connected with her to share their experiences, and eventually with a writer for *Jezebel* who reported out the story in alarming detail.

All say they'd been subjected to sex that wasn't consensual, and to "unwanted physical violence"—as distinct from *wanted* physical violence, though they all seemed to waver, as things were unfolding, about where the line was. The guy had asked one woman in advance if she was into rough sex, and perhaps she was, though not in the way he went about it—she woke up feeling like an anvil had been dropped on her and covered with bruises. She said she confronted him and he said it wouldn't happen again, so she ended up staying at his apartment and watching television the next day. With the others he just proceeded, they allege, hitting and punching during sex, including in the face. One woman says he choked her until she passed out. He forced sex on others after they said no, they say, including without a condom, necessitating at least one trip to the pharmacy for Plan B the following day. One said he forced her to do coke during sex. He demanded blow jobs but wouldn't reciprocate, and much other contemptible conduct.

After which—and this I found upsetting and befuddling—they all continued seeing him, leaving his apartment bruised and battered, then hooking up with him again multiple times, returning for consensual sex even after being hit or raped, they allege, and maintaining friendly contact over months or years. It's like they were superglued to him. When he moved to the West Coast Helen went out to visit him, after which he texted to say their relationship wasn't working out. She said he needed to apologize for assaulting her; he said she'd bruised because she was anemic. Another woman convinced herself she had a crush on him even after he'd forced her into sex after she said no; she later told him she didn't want to just be a "fling" anymore and tried to get him to commit to something more serious. A woman who alleged he'd choked and punched her said he'd text after midnight and ask her to come over; when she said "yes," he'd say "never mind." This went on for a couple of months—he seemed to get off on emotional sadism too. It was only later, after hearing the others' stories, that they each started reevaluating what had happened to them and whether they'd actually consented to any of it.

As far as I could tell this guy had no social power to leverage other than being cute in a Bushwick (neon-colored shorts and Hawaiian shoes) sort of way. He could be charming and complimentary, he'd been published, but it's not like he was running a movie studio. It's more like the women themselves were conferring some imaginary power on him that he didn't actually have. It's as though they endowed him with the phallus, treated him almost as though he were magical. As though being with him conferred some value on them by proximity. The irony, if I can fall back on that overused word, is that the guy had briefly written a series of columns about male feminism for an online site (these were apparently in a parodic vein), though his byline seems to have appeared nowhere since he was outed as a serial abuser.

Why did these women keep going back to him? It doesn't seem to have been pleasure or anything close. They were all savvy, "liberated," schooled—one infers, given the demographic—in contemporary feminism and its rowdy online iterations. Yes, there was drinking and coke involved, some said, meaning impaired thinking and judgment, meaning sometimes the terrible sex was only half remembered. But what exactly was his draw? In past decades the term "masochism" might have been invoked, but that's out of fashion lately—his apparent hatred of women is what we should be talking about, and a culture that tolerates it, according to the current conversation. If you want to get psychological, a staple explanation in online feminism is that women sometimes end up in abusive situations because they've suffered abuse in the past, and Helen said this was true in her case, which helped explain why she'd been in denial about what was going on with him and how bad it was. Yet all the women also overvalued his company and attentions in ways that demand more explanation, not that I have a great one at the ready.

Did they confuse abuse and love? Are single male writers such a scarce commodity in Brooklyn that they get sexual carte blanche, even for sexual violence? Does scarcity produce love? There's something difficult to talk about when it comes to heterosexuality and its abjections, that's always been too complicated (Andrea Dworkin—*Intercourse*—is great on the abjections but couldn't get her head around the pleasures), and #MeToo has in no way made talking about it any more honest. I suspect that the most politically awkward libidinal position for a young woman at the moment would be a sexual attraction to male power. BDSM has the advantage of theatricalizing dominance and submission—you can role-play and not have to look at things too deeply, even if sometimes playing around with violence in bed isn't just playing around. It's a truism that we attract and are attracted to people whose histories chime with our own, and maybe not always in the most benign ways. We all know the slasher film convention: A lone woman goes into a deserted house where the psycho killer awaits. "Don't go in the house!" the audience screams. The phrase itself was the title of a 1979 film about a deranged maniac who'd been abused as a child by a sadistic mother who tried to "burn the evil out of him." Now he subjects women to the same treatment. A practical problem to consider when deciding which Bushwick hipster-writer to go home with is that there are probably as many damaged men out there as there are abused women.

A difficult question: If guys with no discernible social power (no Kissinger quotient whatsoever) and little evident short-term upside remain the beneficiaries of the bad old hierarchies, who exactly is still enforcing them? I suppose it's easier to focus on the considerable ways that men are shitheads and abusers than the considerable ways that we ourselves prop them up. By "we," I include myself. If it's going to be #TimesUp on the shitheadery, if the political demand of the moment is for men to give up the toxic masculinity and toxic sexual behaviors, are there vestigial aspects of femininity that should perhaps be on the chopping block too?*

There's a built-in weirdness to possessing a sexuality, whatever your gender. It reminds us that we're animals; it's bendable into perverse antisocial configurations, which is probably something we also like about it. It's not exactly news that sexuality fractures self-coherence. We're badly held together by social mores and the threat of punishment, which is how we become such good compartmentalizers. We're afflicted with bizarre amoral dreams on a nightly basis. Our fantasy lives don't always comport with progressive ideas about who we should be. You go to work and have to pretend you don't have genitals under your clothes, and that your coworkers don't

---

* I wasn't the only one fascinated by this story. A mini-scandal broke out in the art world in 2019 when a feminist artist exhibited a large installation piece about #MeToo titled "Open Secret," at Art Basel, appropriating—without consent—the bruised selfies Helen had tweeted. Helen responded vitriolically, via Twitter, indicting the commodification of her trauma "for rich ppl to gawk at." Even *Top Chef* host Padma Lakshmi weighed in, condemning the installation. The idea that you can own or control what you put on the internet seems as likely to succeed as a relationship with an abusive male feminist.

either. Some say "keeping it zipped" is more of a problem for natal men, given a physiology that externalizes desires more blatantly; humans without penises are (some say) less beset. But women can be weirdos and sadists too: the worst fictions about us are that our natures are pacific and oppression has made us nobler people. Online feminism is itself a playground of bullying and viperishness, most of it under the banner of rectitude.

A question the #MeToo conversation tends to evade is the degree to which compulsive sexuality of the encroaching sort is always entirely a "choice." Among the newsflashes of the last few years has been the astounding seriality of the harassment enterprise, the enormous numbers of victims so many of the harassers racked up. It's like they were programmed by some invisible hand to extract sex—or revenge, or humiliation, or whatever—from unwilling women (in a few cases, unwilling teenage boys). Whatever the perps were after, clearly no quantity of it ever sufficed. If sexual domination assuages something for certain men, and extracting sexual compliance is some form of recompense, it's clearly a temporary solution at best; you'll soon need another fix. Learning about other humans acting so robotically presents a conceptual difficulty. We wish to emphasize the moral agency of the predators and their supposed gains—the sadistic pleasure, the glee of getting away with it—which enlarges their monstrosity and distinguishes them from the rest of us. But who would "choose" to be a robot?

Some years ago I had coffee with a man who had Tourette's, and whose tic involved touching, which meant that he kept leaning across the small table and touching me on the shoulder, eventually migrating to the breast area. It made me uncomfortable, but I didn't want to mention it because I didn't know if he could control it. Was it lechery or disability? A similar question nags about various of the sexual malefactors in the news. Anthony Weiner had the honor, for many years, of being the public face of the sexual tic—his name helped, of course. Here was a man of demonstrable intelligence under the sway of a compulsion so intellectually disabling that after a string of previous life-wrecking exposures, he still allowed himself to be set up once again, this time by a fifteen-year-old girl, to whom he sent a bunch of dick pics. Something propelled him onto the path most likely to result in massive public humiliation. What sort of problem was this a solution to? Anyone could have seen from ten miles away that it was a frame (the teenager later confessed that she was trying to influence the course of the 2016 presidential election—Weiner's wife worked for Hillary Clinton—and probably succeeded). Anyone could have seen it but Weiner, that is.

Then came COVID and even under lockdown men *still* wanted to violate boundaries, crashing Zoom sessions, jumping off your screen into your kitchen or bedroom, still waving those precious dicks around like sabers, if not always intentionally. Compounded by the fact that legions of us were working at home—cue the *New Yorker* cartoons about people in business casual from shoulders up and underwear down below. Then *The New Yorker*'s esteemed legal correspondent, Jeffrey Toobin, managed to immolate his career on a Zoom session, exposing himself to his colleagues, and thus to that avenging sword of justice known as the H.R. department. At work on a podcast about the then-upcoming 2020 election with a number of well-known journalists, and while others were convening in breakout rooms, Toobin took a second video call (a sex call, presumably). Not realizing he was still on camera with his colleagues, he was next observed taking out his penis and masturbating, lowering his computer to lap level to capture the action for someone. Which, needless to say, became an instant international scandal. His colleagues didn't have to leak it to the media, they *were* the media.

Yes, this was spectacularly stupid. Still, no one on the work call was being asked to *participate;* Toobin wasn't a subway flasher using them to get off. One suspects that no one in this assemblage of media sophisticates would, if polled, condemn masturbation. Everyone was at a safe enough distance, miles from the scene of the crime, yet some (according to blind quotes in other outlets) felt contaminated nonetheless. Even one of his queer colleagues initially described the incident as "traumatic." And the trauma was . . . what exactly? The sight of a colleague's penis? Knowing that he was the sort of sex fiend who masturbates during daylight hours? What a paltry

form of queerness, minus all the Eros and social contestation!
Toobin quickly entered the pantheon of toxic men and parole
from this condition is rare. He was fired from *The New
Yorker* (where he'd been a staff writer for twenty-seven years)
to the delight of the online fulminators—as with Anthony
Weiner his name now seemed too prophetic: #Toobingate
became the favored hashtag.

On the justice of this response, left and right could agree,
bipartisanship at last. *National Review:* "It should not be
an unreasonably high standard to ask people not to engage
in sex acts while talking to their work colleagues." A noted
feminist's Twitter feed described what Toobin had done as
sexual assault and her followers roundly concurred. It was
"perverted," said one. Someone else said if she'd been in the
meeting she'd have felt assaulted "not by the actual incident
but by the thought that he was masturbating while in a meeting with me." A self-described H.R. consultant declared it
"sexual harassment to the highest degree." Others said, "I
honestly never even DREAMED that being on Zoom was not
a safe space." "I'm sad and so angry. The hatred of women
runs so deep." One person kept thinking about "the trauma
inflicted on everyone in that meeting. I can't imagine it. They
may laugh it off, but this kind of thing is very damaging."
Some disputed that it was a mistake—"No one is 'accidentally caught' if they're doing it outside their own homes"—so
addled by the episode she'd managed to forget that people
actually were working from home these days.

A male friend said that if the penis were a better-looking organ, it wouldn't have been such a big deal. Or perhaps if the camera had caught Toobin having a nooner with his wife. For my part, I didn't get how whipping yourself into a lather of moral indignation about someone beating off on a Zoom call wasn't as self-stroking as beating off on a Zoom call, but no doubt my relation to the phallus is as confused as anyone's. Or maybe I mean the penis. Either way, is this to be #MeToo's legacy, that the very thought of a masturbating man spells trauma? That sexuality is such a dangerous contaminant that inadvertent and momentary displays of it are career-ending? What's radical about this, except nothing?*

Revolutions always contain both radical and conservative elements, and the conservative elements of #MeToo—the H.R. department *jeu d'esprit*—have pretty much hijacked whatever was once grassroots and profound. Employers deploy it to seize more power over workers' lives than nineteenth-century factory owners ever dreamed of. Women take to the fainting couch when thinking about someone *else's* sighting of a penis. Masturbation is such a contagion that the idea of it happening on the other side of town affronts. Here were purported feminists, avowed queers, and liberal media bigwigs, united in the pietism that our new pandemic

---

* After eight months in the stockades, Toobin was allowed back on the air at CNN (where he'd been chief legal analyst), though only after apologizing on air for being "deeply moronic" and "a flawed human being."

workspaces—which frequently doubled as our bedrooms, conditions we were all struggling to adapt to—should be as sanctified as churches.

Contamination fears and purity tests had, of course, been sweeping our ostensibly left-wing campuses long before the pandemic hit, and weaponized trauma had reached pandemic proportions itself. I liked things much better when it was the right who treated sex as dangerous, laughably fixated on sin and shame. It used to be conservatives who were the virtue-mongers, but the new ones are swinging and swapping mates, all about insurrection and breaking things, cackling with malevolent self-delight like Heath Ledger's Joker. Even the evangelicals! Somehow they're the ids and transgressors, now it's the "social justice left" who are the superegos, playing the stiffs and sticks-up-the-ass. (By "social justice left" I do not mean the *socialist* or *democratic left* who are a different breed; my own affinities lie in the latter camps.) Needless to say, each side has its favorite pollutant, its signature purity campaigns, and every purity campaign needs a contaminant to eliminate. For the campus social justice crowd it's sexual predators, for the right, immigrants (for the fringe right, Democrat-pedophiles); equally mythologized figures, equally invaders to be vanquished.

What this will mean for post-COVID higher ed is nothing good, I suspect. The carceral campus is a joyless, fearful, anti-intellectual place. Students have developed quite an affinity for turning in their professors to higher-ups, and campuses keep hiring more staff to solicit the accusations. Like the corporate workplaces they increasingly emulate, here too Eros has been mutilated and evacuated. No one can be spotless enough, making these grim locales for us who work there, like *Survivor* for the bookish and out of shape. I love my students, who can be funny and imaginative, but there's a whole lot of sanctimoniousness woven into the mantras of neoliberal wokeness. One detects a certain murderous will-to-power beneath the sanctimonies. We all now fear setting off the social justice goons—by "we" I mean leftist, queer, and trans professors included (some think we're the ones most targeted). You keep hearing the phrase "it's generational"— code for millennials wanting to euthanize their elders. Understandably, we came of age in better times. Also a few of us still cling to outmoded ideas about intellectual freedom, or can be irreverent about the wrong things, like sex. For such errors our jobs are not infrequently on the line.

Gender on campus is ever more a smorgasbord of options, reminiscent of what sex was to previous eras: a new hill to die on. The general idea is that the male-female binary, long our foundational way of organizing the world (to paraphrase trans theorist Jack Halberstam), has run out of steam, with trans and nonbinary people emerging as moral avatars for a regendered future. I'm all for experimentation and gender rebellions of any stripe, though as a lapsed Marxist-feminist

I sometimes find myself wondering: if consumer capitalism's signature loyalty program is the illusion of free choice and there are seventy-one different gender options on Facebook, are these unrelated things? Gender has always been an invention, and if it's now no longer a destiny but a shopping mall, it's still a social invention. (Okay, the jury remains out—"born this way" concepts have their adherents, ranging from evolutionary psychologists to sectors of the trans community.)

Personally, I'd be more excited about the possibilities of bespoke gender identities if the new versions of human freedom being imagined in gender-nonconforming neighborhoods were slightly less rigid. Slightly less invested in policing everyone else. Once upon a time, queers were anti-normative! It was kind of the point! That's not exactly the case anymore. If you want to see some old-school shaming in action, try nonbinary Twitter, where a special form of viciousness is reserved for trans people who decide to medically transition. In other words, the price for the wrong kind of genderqueerness is being subjected to the very punishments—shaming and pathologizing, the threat of violence and exposure—you'd think a self-respecting social renegade would wish to abolish. It's like an anti–capital punishment group leveling death sentences on deviationist allies, or if so-called "pro-lifers" wanted to execute women who have abortions. (Oh wait, they do.) It's not hard to see that a sense of vulnerability might express itself in linguistic rigidities, or that familiarity with being shamed could shade into a comfort level with shaming dynamics generally. Vulnerability calcified into aggression is hardly an unfamiliar move—in the political register it's often said about Zionists, to pick just one of many available examples. In the gender sphere it's traditionally been the hallmark of sovereign masculinity.

And thus do we become our enemies, mirroring our opponents' idiocies.

Where campus life and the larger culture converge is the shared premise that sexual danger abounds in social nooks and crannies that were once mistakenly regarded as harmless. Meaning that when *Teen Vogue,* lately a progressive touchstone, ran a story early in the pandemic about how to have great online sex—the idea being that you could socially distance and still hook up—it wasn't about pleasure, which would have sounded antiquated. No, the entire article was about the various kinds of harm that could be inflicted in digital spaces, and how to increase your virtual safety. Perils are everywhere and somehow new ones keep having to be thought up.

As mentioned, one of those new perils is intergenerational desire, and not just women are at risk from it; teenage boys too are prone to trauma should they become the object of an older person's attentions or desires, including women teachers and attractive neighbors. The same people once extolled and sentimentalized for initiating awkward young men into sex are now getting imprisoned and labeled perverts for it. I suppose you can count the invention of the female predator as progress of a sort, if you felt (as I do) that the social conversation had been getting a little smug about the female virtues.

One such predator was the actress-director Asia Argento, propelled from the status of #MeToo luminary (she was one of Harvey Weinstein's first accusers) to #MeToo archvillainess after being accused of having sex with a seventeen-year-old actor named Jimmy Bennett. She was thirty-seven at the time. Bennett had previously monetized their one sexual interaction into a $380K settlement, which Argento called a shakedown. (First he demanded a payoff then exposed her—isn't it supposed to be one or the other?) He'd been triggered, he said, by Argento's claim to have been sexually victimized by Harvey Weinstein—he seemed to regard her victim status as somehow impinging on his. He said she'd gotten him drunk in a hotel room in California, then forced him to have sex; she initially denied the sex, then said he was the one who aggressed on her—her story kept changing, which didn't look good, though both accounts had their inconsistencies. (As do age-of-consent laws—if the two had had sex in Nevada, the next state over where the consent age is sixteen, it would have been technically legal at least.)

On Twitter, Argento wasn't just a sex predator, she was now said to have caused her boyfriend Anthony Bourdain's suicide by involving him in the payoff to Bennett. As you'd expect, the gender reversal lent extra malice to the proceedings. Though a seventeen-year-old and a thirty-seven-year-old in bed may now appall, recall that a couple of generations ago the play *Tea and Sympathy*—which concludes with the sexual proposition of a prep school student by his headmaster's wife—was a sentimental Broadway hit. There was even a 2007 off-Broadway revival. Knowing that the boundaries of what's acceptable and what isn't keep jumping around and reversing, shouldn't moral pronouncements come with more humility, not wrapped in the cloak of timeless universality?

Of course, there *are* a few timeless themes, and one is the terror of sexual mother-monsters. Argento had once played Bennett's mother on-screen, in a movie she also directed, hence some of the disgust directed at her, one imagines. Movie mom and son in bed is far too close to incest, the biggest of the taboos, though would incest need to be taboo if we didn't also at some level desire it? Who knows? The point is that morally acceptable seduction stories operate on one vector only at the moment: me victim, you abuser. Me chaste, you sex fiend. For my part I wonder what it feels like to slay the flamboyant-admired-loathed-loved monster-mentor with the sharp sword of a demand letter or a public exposé. To rob then publicly butcher the temptress mother, leaving her bleeding and destroyed. Does it feel good? That must be part of the story too—just not the part that can be monetized.

Closer to my own world is the fiftyish woman professor who wrote me during the pandemic, having lost everything over a kiss she herself didn't even initiate. At least this was her account of events, after the male undergrad she said had kissed *her* turned her in. The student had been intellectually brilliant, a sort of wunderkind, more like a grad student in terms of intellectual sophistication. And looked a lot older. The two of them had gotten close, too close obviously, even though it was only intellectually, but that meant they were behaving like friends, having meals together off-campus, cooking dinner together at her house when she was his adviser on a summer research project. Which was where he came onto her unexpectedly. They kissed for about ten minutes, then they both freaked out and she drove him home.

Maybe that would have been the end of the story, except that she wanted to have a conversation with him and make sure things were okay, but he refused to respond to her for three weeks, other than an irate string of text messages. She freaked out and sent a long string of messages in response—nothing in any way sexual, but she did say she loved him, which she meant in a purely platonic way, and she *did* feel a real enduring love for him. Which is what hung her in the end—putting that to paper (as it were).

After three weeks of ghosting her he finally reappeared, and they talked for hours in her office and things seemed to have been worked out between them. They went back to a more proper relationship. He took a class with her in the fall. Everything seemed fine, until his mental demons began resurfacing. Her brilliant student turned out to be unstable, drinking to excess and she said, unable to write the papers he needed to write to graduate. He wrote her a long email saying that he hated her due to his own self-hatred about his failures, and the fact that she'd achieved everything he wanted for himself and now would never have. None of which was due to the kiss, he acknowledged.

But a few months later, doing badly in multiple courses, he changed his mind, and with a blackmailer's artfulness said he wanted a passing grade for a class with her for which he'd done no work. She refused. He finally turned in the work a few hours before grades were due and she gave him an A but he failed his other classes and couldn't graduate on time. At which point he decided that the trauma of the kiss—though by now a year had passed—had caused the problems, and he filed a complaint, saying she'd pressured him to drink (she says she doesn't even drink). As for the kiss, he was a foot taller, it's not like she could have overpowered him.

In retrospect she realized she'd been tragically naïve, made terrible judgment mistakes, and crossed boundaries that should not have been crossed. She was mortified at herself. The worst thing was the sense of shame at being a middle-aged woman accused of harassing an undergrad, exactly because men are supposed to be the aggressors and power brokers. Middle-aged women are meant to be safe and sexless. Everywhere on campus gender binaries are being challenged and queerness reigns—embraced by the institutions! established in the curriculum!—except that sexualized mothers are as much of a threat (or joke) as ever. The reality was that she was a single mother whose kids' welfare was entirely dependent on her and she'd soon be out of a job. She'd started thinking of her student's motives as like a murder-suicide pact: he couldn't have what she had so decided to take her, the person he'd once been closest to, down with him. Her (female) supervisor's view was that the text messages she'd sent, pointing out to her student that he'd been the one to initiate the kiss, had been written to proleptically revise the narrative in the event of a future investigation. It was foreordained that she was guilty and needed to be terminated.

The question you'd want to ask the supervisor and other higher-ups is what deadly form of contamination they thought had been transmitted in those brief moments of lip-to-lip contact? Maybe I'm a hopeless sentimentalist but it sounded to me as though the two of them did love each other, but it was a love so prohibited it had to end in banishment. The student had to reimagine that his teacher's lips on his, which he'd desired himself—perhaps conflictedly—had harmed him to such an extent that her career and future penury (and that of her kids) were the reparations he deserved.

We all know the truisms about the proximity of love and hate, and daring to love someone opens those portals. You can get sucked in, obliterated, spat out, and not even understand what happened.

—

No one's hands can be clean enough. We're fighting contagions on every front—moral, viral, sexual. Which will mean what, in the years to come, post-plague, when and if things finally go back to usual, for the texture of our lives, our loves, our bodily propinquities?

Conveniently for the narrative arc of his eventual biopic, the sexually monstrous Harvey Weinstein would be among the first male luminaries to test positive for COVID—this was after his conviction and remand to Rikers, but he was already the Patient Zero of a plague, the international plague of sexual predators. Donald Trump, then still in office, was blithely killing off the citizenry as blithely as he'd grabbed pussies in Before Times; gratifyingly Trump got infected too, a biohazard at every level. He made a miraculously quick recovery, unlike the country. After his bout with the virus one of his troll sons tweeted this bizarre fantasy: "Imagine this. Trump gets better and donates his plasma to develop a corona treatment. And then all the liberals will have to get vaccinated with Trump's blood."

As the pandemic dragged on, as we locked down, crept out, re-distanced, and got vaccinated, even as deadly new variants struck, I'd started noticing essays and social media aperçus—usually by women, presumably single—waxing nostalgic about the touch of strangers in bars. They wanted to be surprised, taken off guard. Touched. Yes, touched! What had been missing from our stripped-down lives was the wildcard element of sex, the disruption to your equilibrium and orderliness. The unpredictability.

Could the pandemic turn out to be a reset, a chance to wipe the bogeyman and -woman from the social imagination, invent wilder, more magnanimous ways of living and loving as we go forward into whatever comes next? I hope this might be true. I understand the difficulties and suspicions. The poet and classicist Anne Carson summarized the dilemma elegantly: "As members of human society, perhaps the most difficult task we face daily is that of touching one another—whether the touch is physical, moral, emotional or imaginary. Contact is crisis."

3

LOVE ON THE ROCKS: "CODEPENDENCY" AND ITS VICISSITUDES

If only there were a nasal swab test for relationship health, given the many pernicious love ailments going around. Among the most worrisome is "codependency," which has reached epidemic proportions despite no one entirely agreeing on what it is. The presenting symptoms include everything from excess clinginess, to covertly fostering your loved one's substance problems because you need to be needed, to not knowing what you feel about things. Conceptual uncertainties notwithstanding, it's had its own Twelve-Step program since 1986. Some claim it's related to that other amorphous and equally ill-defined modern malady, *narcissism*—indeed, narcissists are said to be natural magnets for codependent personality types, who are then further tarred as "co-narcissists."

You can probably tell that I'm dubious (or possibly resentful) about such overconfident diagnoses, though the endless months of compulsory coupled domesticity definitely had me pondering them. Everyone needs a theory of coupled pathology these days, even a cheesy one, like needing a lifeline after you've fallen into a hidden well. Codependency explains why coupledom has made you unrecognizable to yourself—it's because your identity has merged with an alien being's, like Jeff Goldblum in *The Fly*. Yet (and though I've studied the matter closely) it remains unclear to me whether you catch codependency *from* your relationship, or you were codependent-prone to begin with and twisted what could have been a "healthy" relationship into an interpersonal trainwreck because of some infernal need to control everyone around you, or your lack of an inner core, or something equally hideous. Or maybe it's not your individual problem, maybe there's just some environmental illness or detrimental alchemy afflicting modern relationships causing boundaries to become spongy and ineffectual, making the question of where one person stops and the other starts an inevitable neurotic tangle.

Or did you accidentally wind up with a drunk, as happened to codependency's most ardent popularizer, Melody Beattie, who married a supposed former alcoholic (himself a respected alcoholism counselor), then found out he'd been lying about not drinking and hadn't been sober since before their marriage. It was a fruitful revelation, generating some fifteen books since the mid-1980s which have sold millions of copies, maybe even tens of millions—the first, *Codependent No More,* was parked on the *New York Times* best-seller list for two years. All around the world people exclaimed "Yes, that's me" and they exclaimed it in twenty languages. We're talking about an international yet puzzlingly vague disorder in the sphere of love, though can it ever be cured when it can barely be defined?

My friend Mason insisted it could. "Sometimes you just have to let them hit bottom," he said via Zoom, talking about his breakup with his wife of over twenty years. I hadn't known she was a drinker ("a mean drunk," as he put it)—in fact I'd never actually met her as he and I weren't really that close, but this was the sort of conversation you found yourself having during the plague months (confessional, painful) because screens made everyone so proximate, and people were feeling emotionally shaken to various degrees and needed to expel things. I'd been noticing friends like Mason, formerly known for irony and insouciance, embracing "codependency" as a relationship heuristic, espousing podcasts featuring celebrity therapists and recommending books with words like "courage" and "change" in the titles. Or possibly they were just recommending them to me, for reasons that will become clear.

Since I'd been thinking about this codependency thing myself, I was attempting to float my theory on the subject to Mason, who was (annoyingly) resisting. I wanted to get him to admit that whatever it meant, it was actually the basic structure of "normal" coupledom, and all long-term relationships invariably devolve into this condition, something that had certainly become more pronounced in pandemic times with couple members thrust together in such cloistered hothouse situations, regardless of the square footage of the bunkers. Don't you invariably wind up complicit in the other person's forms of stuckness, whatever they are? They say we're hardwired to mimic those we love, to synchronize our expressions and emotions with our lovers, to "catch" each other's moods, even when things are going well.

Now we were all bleeding into each other in ways that could be toxic and maybe sometimes curative or possibly both at once, but obviously the closer you are to someone the more porous you are. Skin isn't a thick enough barrier to stanch the avalanche of blood and guts inside. The more vulnerable you are, the more damage you do and gets done to you in turn. If you stab someone—yes, it was *absolutely* self-defense, you're *totally* off the hook—they're going to hemorrhage all over the furniture however much they deserved it, and you're the one left cleaning up the mess. Sorry, I'm being metaphorical—I'm trying to talk about "feelings" and what flimsy defenses any of us ultimately has against the roiling chaos of our partner's inner life under confinement, simultaneously each other's enablers and projection screens. I suppose some relationships were made stronger, got closer. Others of us were left mopping up the spillage.

The general point I was attempting to make to Mason is that the things you think you most despise or despair of, or hold in secret contempt about your mate, you also, in some covert fashion, foster and facilitate.

Some trace the source of the codependency concept to

the pioneering early psychoanalyst Karen Horney, a critic of Freud (she didn't buy the penis envy thing), who emigrated from Germany to the U.S. and wrote, among a multitude of papers and books on neurotic coupledom, "The Overvaluation of Love. A Study of a Common Present-Day Feminine Type," the original better version of the *Women Who Love Too Much* syndrome. (This was another mid-1980s iteration of codependency theory that became an international best seller.) Horney's 1933 article still rings uncomfortably true, perhaps because she turns out to have been one of the breed herself, having had a lengthy tormented love affair with the left-wing Freudian Erich Fromm, fifteen years her junior, who'd later write *The Art of Loving* in 1956, though he seems to have been less than artful at it himself.

Fromm always sounds like Mr. Admirable Humanist when he waxes on about "freedom" and "relatedness," but he was an ambivalent shit to Horney which she wrote about pseudonymously in her book *Self-Analysis,* under the guises of "Claire" and "Peter." After a lot of self-flagellation, Claire finally realizes that she's morbidly dependent on men and must get over it, but what of Peter? Did *he* ever wonder why he was so unavailable, keeping Claire at a distance while assuring her that he loved her, canceling vacation plans at the last minute then berating her for being upset, stringing her along for years with broken promises before finally ditching her for someone else? (Horney later retaliated by getting him kicked out of the psychoanalytic institute she headed, purportedly because he lacked an M.D. though the whiff of payback lingers. Which I hope she at least enjoyed.)

I guess we write about what we can't figure out or are hopeless at, one thing that draws me to Horney on love, also her quip that people go into therapy to perfect their neuroses, not abandon them.

Via Zoom, Mason maintained that what *he* meant by codependence was specific to life with an alcoholic (it emerged his ex was also a pillhead and a rageaholic, she covered all the bases). It was the structure of coupledom with a substance abuser he was talking about. Who doesn't have "substance issues," I rejoined, thinking of all the things people manage to addict themselves to (pot, cake, porn, video games). And all the non-substantive substances—maybe it's emotional turmoil they can't get enough of, or avoidance, or pathological perfectionism (a.k.a. writer's block). Whatever the particulars, you, the partner, are left with an array of unsatisfactory options in response: you're in denial, or you're the "fixer," or you jump ship.

Though not a couple, Mason and I were already in the throes of a couple quarrel. We weren't just arguing theoretically about the manner in which entrenched couple dynamics unfold, we were having the kind of quarrel warring couples have, that is, if you think, as I do, that couples are defined more by the form of their arguments than the content. Which usually means wanting something from the other person they're just not going to give you, because they're insisting on their own reality. *Here is life according to me. Here's a list of my needs. That you have not met.* Which is coupledom in a nutshell, and also the shape of our current quarrel: I was a coupledom formalist, he was married to his specifics. We both secretly thought the other person was missing the point. We could probably have this argument for a lifetime.

His view was that his wife had been "a fucking drunk" who'd eventually cratered and hit bottom to the point that everything necessarily blew up, finally propelling him out of the marriage for good. But without the accelerant of alcohol, he said, you're talking about very different things. If his wife had hit bottom earlier and dealt with her alcoholism earlier, maybe they'd still be married. I was after a grander theory, a bigger insight, and he wasn't going to give it to me. We wanted different things from each other. What he wanted from me (I inferred, possibly incorrectly) was an audience for grisly stories about his marriage which he told with much creative flourish, doing all the voices (he was a hilarious mimic, which I'd never known), sending me into peals of mordant laughter. (The laughter of uncomfortable recognition some percentage of the time.) He did his wife in a biting accusatory falsetto and himself in a whiny whimper, mocking the contemptuous chump he obviously thought he'd been for too many years, his voice quivering like a violin vibrato—"This is the *last* time. I'm going to *find. Another hidden bottle.*" It was a boozy Punch and Judy show with his ex as Mr. Punch, and me a furtive spectator on someone else's inner pandemonium. (Which was at least a relief from my own.)

The agenda, I sensed, was reconfirming for himself that he'd been right to fly the coop, that he was a good guy in spite of it, and maybe I should think about getting out of my own situation too, to the extent that "codependency" (he sensed) was its emotional tenor. Leaving had been brutal for him, and the most brutal thing was that he had to do it to save his own life. But saving his life was also a self-inflicted wound, an evisceration. He'd loved his wife, loved her deeply. Leaving was loneliness and horror and guilt. He intimated that I wanted to rewrite the larger codependency narrative in the manner I did to deflect attention from having to think about my own story, to not "face things." I intimated that he felt he needed to justify himself to me, which he didn't. I wasn't judging him, it's not like I'm in any position to judge anyone's relationship choices. I thought his definition of codependence was too tailored to his own situation; he thought mine was too global. (Yes I like my theories on a global scale, that's my form of grandiosity. Get me to a support group.)

What *he* meant by codependence was that he'd been susceptible to "emotional" (as opposed to sexual) affairs from the early stages of his marriage, he admitted, even before his wife had started drinking—she hadn't started boozing until her twenties, but then quickly made up for lost time. (We had in common that our mates weren't drinkers at the beginning, it wasn't what we'd signed up for. A note of mutual grievance crept into our voices recounting these forked histories.) Still, he thought of his wife as the addictive personality, not himself. When she drank, she drank like a college kid, to obliteration. Early on, he'd say, "Wow, you really got fucked up last night"—it wasn't wow, this person has a problem. And you don't foresee getting addicted to someone else's problem until you do. You have good boundaries until you don't. You don't anticipate the ways that love will change you, fasten you to a person, what it can habituate you to. Or turn you into. Witness Mason—he wasn't a quitter, yet this time he'd quit. I could see the toll the breakup had taken on his core self-definition, and that he was still in the process of reconstructing the story of who he was. He'd never run out of gas before, then he ran out of gas. So who was he now?

Listening to the details of someone else getting derailed by love was somehow comforting. I like stories about love's grisly side. So did one of the women psychoanalytic patients Karen Horney describes in "The Overvaluation of Love," who at the beginning of her treatment kept sending Horney flowers, at first anonymously and then openly. Under analysis, she acknowledged fantasizing that the presents would make Horney dependent on her, but it was a fantasy with a deeper destructive meaning. "She would like, she said, to be my maid and do everything for me to perfection. Thus I would become dependent upon her, trust her completely, and then one day she would put poison in my coffee." It's a fantasy, says Horney, typical of those who overvalue love—"Love is a means of murder."

But that's the thing—who *doesn't* overvalue love? Why else had Mason stayed as long as he had? The coffee had been poisoned long ago. Now he was looking back on his relationship history, thinking about that long-standing pattern of emotional affairs, and trying to be honest with himself about the codependency element. The problem had been that his wife's drunken accusations and shaming had accelerated his need for love and corroboration, and he was a guy women had always liked and felt at ease talking to—good-looking, funny and successful—so these kinds of relationships were popping up right and left. Which he seized on to feel better about himself. None of which surprised me; I noticed he had a quasi-seductive way of saying your name in conversation, reminding you that he was thinking of you, not just of himself (not that I'm in any way susceptible to that sort of thing). The platonic affairs had been a sort of unconscious space he created for himself in the marriage. You just get so fucking desperate for some joy, he said sadly. Some of the friendships maybe got a little intense, but for a long time the sexual component was so tame as to be junior high (I didn't remind him that these days junior high schoolers are posting about anal on their Insta accounts).

Except soon the affairs became a sort of addiction, this "please love me" imperative kind of took over, and like every other substance-reliant citizen of the planet, it started to be how he organized his time. He'd look forward to occasions his wife might be away so he could cook dinner for the current semi-platonic pal, even if they didn't end up naked in bed—okay, maybe some making out, but no bodice-ripper sort of thing. He admitted having had a Bill Clinton kind of attitude toward sex, like "it's not really infidelity if I don't stick it in," even though he recognized the distinction was ridiculous and thought of Clinton as a sleaze. And he didn't, for a long time, stick it in, not for years, not until things had gotten pretty bad in the marriage, and his wife was drifting further and further into a haze. Recounting this, his tone was tinged with despair. As her life got oriented more and more around drinking, her blindness to that side of him—the emotional affair–needing side—increased, and he felt like she knew him less and less, like a veil was being pulled over her eyes. Of course, he was the one doing the pulling, hiding the emotional affairs and what he got out of them, but whose fault was that? The turn-on for him wasn't being fucked, it was just being *heard*. As her drinking got worse, so did her anger, which upped his need for consolation from other women. The two of them were locked in their separate monadic worlds, but locked in them as husband and wife. On the one hand they were utterly estranged, and on the other excessively merged.

I said it seemed like he thought of "codependency" as a permission slip to do what he was going to do anyway. There was almost an alchemy to it: turning the other person's addiction into the purchase price for your freedom, even as in your mind it's also an anvil weighing you down. It was an interestingly creative strategy, making the mate's symptom work to get what you wanted in the first place. Did I do that myself? There was something perversely encouraging about it, from a certain vantage—the multitude of ways people manage to find corners of freedom even in the most joy-killing situations.

Yet in the marital timeline he was sketching, his emotional affairs had actually long preceded his wife's drinking problem, which he vaguely knew—and wasn't that at odds with the theory of codependence he'd been pitting against mine? In his telling, the more she drank, the more he felt like he was owed something. It was a secret quid pro quo that only he knew about. You start forgetting how to pay attention to your feelings, he said, because so much of you gets subsumed into the managing of this unmanageable thing, the other person's addiction. You forget to ask yourself something as simple as What would I like to do today? As the spouse ever-so-subtly blames you for their problems (or as a good codependent mate you assume responsibility for them unbidden) you start experiencing yourself as harmful, powerful, dangerous. Of course the mate and their addictions are equally a danger to you. Mutual paranoia sets in. In time, his calculation became: I'm just going to *take* certain things, I'm going to *have* that experience, because on my deathbed, having put up with this shit, I'm gonna regret having not done it if I don't.

This was hardly an unfamiliar logic to me. Isn't couple-dom always a form of double-entry bookkeeping, a ledger of debits and credits? Which we know because so many couples dissolve for precisely these reasons, which their friends all hear about, sometimes ad infinitum: *"It's not worth it," "I'm giving more than I'm getting"*—as opposed to happy couples who, by definition, accrue compound interest, banking their love in a joint account, knowing they're richer together than apart.

Which is where the codependency comes in, at least as Mason defined it. You're not really relating to each other, you're looking for subterranean motives and dodging accusations. So maybe some of those emotional affairs become more full-on sexually charged. Yes, soon he was having a bona fide affair, which part of him almost resented his wife for not discovering, but she was so regularly looped by then she didn't notice much of anything.

Was her obliviousness an upside or not? Certainly a partner's drinking gives the non-drunk person the moral edge (and did we not get a teensy bit of enjoyment from our martyrdom, what morally superior being doesn't?), but he was squandering his in sin. It's not like having an affair made him feel *good* about himself. It's not like he didn't recognize the absurdity of blaming his wife for not noticing that he was having an affair that he himself was actively concealing from her. But he blamed her all the same, which is as codependent as it gets, he self-indicted.

I said that my understanding of how people generally use the term "codependency" is that the non-drunk partner *enables* the drinking, like a sort of unconscious bargain, to the point that you're covertly helping the person *stay* lodged in their substance abuse. On the one hand you're counting their drinks, pleading with them to go to meetings, you're the mean mommy snatching away the pacifier. On the other, you're covering up for them at work or in social situations, explaining/lying that they got a sudden attack of flu so unfortunately couldn't make it to the dinner party, when the truth is they're home puking because they're recovering from a binge. Or maybe something in you secretly loves their woundedness, gets addicted to fixing it. *You alone* can make them better through your intelligence and competence and nurturing and psychological acuity. *Things will change for the better. You will cure them.* What more addictive idea is there than that? Also so quintessentially American, or at least Emersonian, this trope of self-invention and reinvention. (Or in its more aggressive rendition, "All right, motherfucker, you're not gonna reinvent yourself? I'm gonna do it for you.") Whereas Mason's version of the syndrome was: I'm putting up with this and I'm going to take that in return. Which I deserve because *look what you're putting me through.*

They're flip sides of the same thing, he said, when I

pointed out that he was being, in my view, contradictory. The most important aspect of codependency, as he meant it, he explained, and the most destructive, is that the person knows you *too fucking well*. They know your foibles, they know you inside and out. Whether or not they remember the insane accusations they made the night before, you're still internalizing it all, internalizing everything, because at some level they know what they're talking about, even when shit-faced. He'd find himself thinking, Yeah, I must really be a bad person, that's why she's a drunk. Yeah, I must really be a really fucking selfish person who never thinks of other people and dominates every dinner conversation, like she said. Part of him knew none of it was true and she was just projecting her self-hatred onto him, she was like a projection machine. But the genius part of codependency is that it may be projection, but it's never entirely untrue either. She'd say things that were tremendously shaming—that he was a failure at things he too worried he was a failure at. That he was a failed man. There were constant beat-downs, and sure she was plastered, but her aim was pretty accurate.

I knew quite well the kind of porousness he was talking about. As they say, "hurt people hurt people," and all the more in pandemic times, with large grievances playing out in small spaces amid the bleakness of interchangeable days. You know the truth is being exaggerated, but you recognize yourself in it and that hooks you very deeply.

Marriage makes you into a liar, he continued bitterly. You

can't let yourself feel what's going on if the relationship is going to survive, so essentially you're lying to yourself all the time. Their substance issues make *you* a liar. You're lying about who you are. You fall into these stupid roles. You're the enforcer. Yeah, you're the surveillance state, I interjected. You're the pill counter, he said, you're measuring the level on the bourbon. The best part of being the surveiller of a lush is that their sense of being surveilled is so dim, he chuckled darkly. Isn't the best part of being a surveiller when you find the evidence? I asked. (Shared knowing laughter.) Yeah, it's like, I'm gonna count your fucking pills, and then I'm gonna bust you. Or, you know, them coming home, you get the kiss. That smells like cigarettes, extra gum, and then just that little whiff of . . . I mean, it's like Proust's madeleines, the smell of bourbon for me now, he said. You become this walking breathalyzer. You get home from being out of town. "Honey, have you slipped? You sounded kind of slurry last night." No goddamnit, I haven't slipped, they say, and then you're tearing the house apart and finding the booze.

What people never talk about: the erotics of finding them out. The creepy satisfaction of it. The little warden-jailbird role-play games couples get up to.

Were you too stumbling on hidden caches during the pandemic months—weird porn, unworn purchases of the same items, unpaid bills, emails to exes, evidence of other secrets? Here's the question when it comes to codependency metrics: Are they hiding it in places where they know you'll find it?

And is that "a cry for help," or brinksmanship? Or are they finding better and better places to hide the stash—in their car, inside of boxes inside of other boxes in the garage—and you've become Sherlock Holmes of the homefront, a total bloodhound? You're not giving up. You both do and don't want to find the secret. On the one hand: success! On the other: shame. You find the evidence, you feel vindicated and pathetic at the same time. No, no, *they're* the pathetic one, but by that point your identities are merged in pathos. You're pathetic because you're looking in the first place, or you're pathetic because you're finding the stash and staying. And if you're staying with someone pathetic, what does that make *you*?

So you mutate into a "fixer," because obviously fixing *their* problem would magically fix your own. And certain gratifications do come with the role: You're vested with the power to forgive or rebuke each binge or relapse, which binds you more closely while also making you a parental figure (not always so great in the bedroom department, but inevitable—when Mason mentioned that his mother occasionally drank too much, I noticed he used the same words he had about his wife: "a mean drunk"). Or you're the angry parent on the phone to their therapist, like, "I want you to know that you're not actually doing anything, you're not helping, you're letting her off the hook. And I want us to come up with some strategies for getting her not to drink anymore." This was Mason, demanding to sit in on a session with his wife's shrink, who afterward turned to him and said "I'm glad you've testified here and that's great, but you really need to think about going to Al-Anon." As if it were *his* problem. As if the two of them were the same person. (Al-Anon is an offshoot of Alcoholics Anonymous, for "people just like you, who are worried about someone with a drinking problem," founded in 1950 by Lois W, wife of A.A. founder Bill Wilson. Anyone involved with an alcoholic will sooner or later be told to go to Al-Anon whether or not the partner is willing to go to A.A. themselves, or says they find A.A. boring because the stories are all the same, the level of cliché is unbearable, and a Thousand Other Reasons.)

And how could it not affect their sex life, Mason said, like there'd be cocktails after work, then they'd have drunken sex which eventually for him started to feel like date rape, which wasn't without its own quotient of self-hatred. He knew it was scummy. But things would unfold, like wow, I'm really horny and my wife's pretty fucked up and I'm not sure she knows who I am right now, but she doesn't care either.

It's not like you're having great sex if one of you is tanked all the time, he said. They'd go to a dinner party and the wine would be flowing and she'd come home and make a bourbon–ginger ale before going to bed and he'd be like, "What are you doing?" Like that's the drink that's gonna kill you tomorrow. Then have half-comatose sex. Or they'd get home from a party and she'd be pissed off about something and launch into one of her blitzkrieg barrages, which is how he started thinking of what happened to the household patois after too much booze, and then there'd be drunken angry sex, again with her half passed out. But it wasn't something they could talk about.

There were these no-go zones, because if he tried to talk about any of it they'd get so fast to a dead-end—and then things would be terrible for the rest of the week. And if he were honest with himself he'd have to get out of the relationship obviously, but by self-definition he wasn't that guy, meaning there were a lot of things he had to collude with himself not to know.

The first affair had been great, but it wasn't going to lead anywhere and it didn't change anything at home. It ended after a year, but it reminded him what sober sex was like: better. He wanted that with his wife. He didn't like the person he'd become. He didn't like the low-level gaslighting it had taken to carry on a long-term affair even when your mate's in a convenient stupor much of the time. By that point their sex life was pretty broken, so the first order of business in the marital repair project was: Let's get her sober. Which was when they first started having talks about "Okay, the drinking is a problem." Talking about the fact that they were more and more emotionally remote. That she was barely relating to him because her primary relationship was with alcohol. But the collateral problem he started being unable to ignore was that by this point the more present he was in the marriage and the more available emotionally, the worse everything felt.

—

The question I wanted to ask was this: If alcoholism is a "disease" according to the current mantra, how do you hold your mate accountable for being a drunk? If it's not your fault you got cancer or diabetes, is it your fault you got drunkenness? If you drive drunk and hit someone you're to blame, not the disease, so says the law. But what about in the courtroom of our relationships: How do you parse what's in your mate's volition and what's a catastrophe foisted on them by alcoholic genes, or family of origin, or a traumatic past? If trauma is ineradicable and the body is a tablet on which every event is written, and someone turns to booze to quell the feelings and becomes a lush . . . what does it mean to be a moral agent under these conditions? Just go to A.A. the non-drunks of the world glibly prescribe, as if A.A. worked. (A.A. says its success rate is 75 percent for people who really try; skeptics say it's in the single digits.) A quarter of people twelve and older binge-drink in any given month—or let's say a quarter of people admit to it. Denial is not unknown in these vicinities. More to the point: Is self-destructiveness volitional? Are you finding a hidden bottle in the garage or are you finding a hidden trauma? Or is putting it that way just making the same tired excuses the mate makes for him- or herself and playing—once again—the chump?

That, Mason said, is "the burden of the partner": the tightrope strung between those two buildings—recognizing it's a disease, but also a responsibility. (Just to be clear, neither of us wanted to give up our own one or two glasses of wine a night—let's not go overboard.) I recalled that the sociologist Ramona Asher, writing about wives in alcohol-affected marriages, uses the term "moral career" to describe how having to make such assessments is one of the disruptive ambivalences of the situation. The codependent spouse doesn't just have to deal with a drunk, you have to restyle yourself as a philosopher of the human condition, like it or not. After seeing his wife go through more than one inpatient rehab, more than one outpatient rehab, and then relapse multiple times, Mason knew it was absolutely a disease. "Neural pathways" have been formed, there are family predispositions, and when someone's been drinking for twenty years that's how they channel so many kinds of feelings . . . "How you self-medicate," I chimed in, coining an entirely fresh phrase. That's the other thing I resent, aside from the obligatory moral career, how you end up spouting a whole thesaurus of recovery clichés, you who once valued your linguistic originality.

You're the wrong kind of person to end up with a drunk, I observed to Mason. He cited Jung about marrying your shadow, your unknown side. Jung can be a dingbat, but I admit he's good on the seductive charms of the overcomplicated mate and how easy it is to lose yourself in their labyrinthine nature. We don't understand the first thing about our motives in mate choice, Jung writes (on this I concur) and it's precisely operating in the dark that gives you that giddy feeling of being "in love." You're veering toward something or someone because . . . why? The more unconscious you are about it, the more you feel you've encountered your true fate. Also people can be deceptive, especially the overcomplicated ones, passing themselves off as simpler than they are at first, splitting off "irreconcilable traits of character," until they've reeled you in and you find yourself increasingly devoted to tracking the twists and turns in your mate's mentality. Which is another reason they're so attractive—you get lost in their layers, which is not disagreeable. Couples are a jungle unto themselves, says Jung, with the simpler personality swallowed up by the more complex personality. To the point that you, the simple one, can't even see your way out, while also unwittingly becoming dependent on your partner's very undependability. (Besides, all the dependable people have started to seem horribly boring by contrast, so what are your options?)

I returned us to the tightrope between the two buildings: *Can* people be other than who they are? *Do* any of us have that choice? Mason thought that however much you see the partner's drinking as a disease it's also impossible, at a relational level, not to hold it against them. Yeah, but then you feel guilty when you do, I observed. That's the cycle—you hold them responsible and let's say feel entitled to have an affair or conduct a secret life, then feel horrible because they're suffering too. They can't help it that they're destroying themselves! Free will? The longer you're coupled with someone the more you realize what a fiction it is, to the extent that coupled intimacy means that a map of someone else's interior life has been sutured onto your own, which can of course feel very gratifying—*closeness, finishing each other's sentences*—and also incredibly stultifying, the more conversant you get with the monotony of someone else's impasses. You know the exact moment their defenses will kick in, or petulance, or temper; you find yourself involuntarily tensing up because your body knows before "you do" when an eruption is coming. Long-term coupledom is like attending the world's most protracted dysfunctional psychology seminar (or maybe living in Kafka's penal colony, except you're being tattooed with the spouse's crimes instead of your own).

Mason said he'd been asking himself lately why he'd gotten divorced. The split was recent enough that he was still constantly thinking back on the marriage, and wondering anew if he could have saved it. Codependency was so braided into their history he still couldn't figure out where his foibles started and hers were just an accelerant on the fire. What finally pushed him over the edge was that he'd always linked his wife's blitzkrieg barrages to her drinking and deeply believed that if she got sober, *when* she got sober, all that would stop, because it was the alcohol speaking, not "her." Except that after one of her final rehabs, when she was sober for nearly a year—she was *exactly the same*. It's not that he thought it was going to be some kind of sober Nirvana, that there would never be hard things to deal with, but he hadn't anticipated the dry drunk thing—all the same issues minus the cushion of booze. Which made the effect of the fights beyond demoralizing—she resented him even more, if that was possible. She'd quit drinking, what had he done for her?

His question finally became: Can I live with what's *not* going to change? After one horrendous scene with her taunting him he nearly lost his shit, he said, and had to quickly walk himself back, terrified that next time—especially after a glass of wine or two—he might haul off and hit her in the mouth and then his life was over. Things were so combative between them she'd more than likely march her ass to a hospital, take some pictures, and he'd never see his kids again.

I knew this kind of spiraling myself, those moments of frightening escalation, knew all about becoming someone in the context of a couple fight you don't even recognize. *That's not me.* Because your boundaries are gone, you've been infused with something malign that hadn't been *in you* previously, that seemed to have spontaneously generated on its own. Or was it actually there all along like those disgusting little maggots you sometimes find in old flour? The FDA allows up to seventy-five or more insect fragments in fifty grams of flour, but are you supposed to sit there and count them? When it gets to be a hundred insect fragments do you throw out the flour? A hundred and ten? Where's the line, what's too much to live with? The line keeps getting crossed, so the line keeps getting moved. And what happens if you leave—are you responsible if they spiral further down and out, as you fear they will? Responsible when they nose-dive? (A worry which in and of itself confirms you, once again, as champ of the enablers.)

His wife would be "You need to go to more Al-Anon meetings." And he was like, "Why, so I can fucking take it?" And that's the thing he resented about Al-Anon, that it's a strategy for taking it. That's the dirty little secret, he said, the thing people don't like to say. *Courage to Change* (an Al-Anon-inspired guide to life with a drunk) recommends treating your alcoholic spouse or family member as a "learning opportunity," since everyone in our lives is also a mirror, reflecting our own better and worse qualities—they can help us work through conflicts from the past that were never resolved. *But isn't that a recipe for codependence in itself?* I thought when I read it myself. *Where are the boundaries supposed to be if you're just each other's mirrors?*

For a while Mason dutifully went to the Al-Anon meetings, where in fact they didn't tell him to "take it"—after the first meeting where he told his story, every guy there came up to him afterward and said some version of, "Hey man, you've got choices." At the time he was like, I don't need some motherfucker telling me I can get out of my marriage. His feeling was, "You're fucking with my resolve. Like I need to find the tools to stay in, not how to get out."

Fast-forward to the present. He'd found that he wasn't entirely displeased to be a divorced heterosexual guy who was aging well and getting more female attention than he could conceivably handle, even in the midst of a pandemic. He wasn't running around like a Tinder-happy freak, but he was adapting to divorced life, and *finally out of the codependence,* which felt weirdly weightless. You get to find parts of yourself you were never able to find before; he marveled at how honest you can finally be. I suggested he pitch a TED Talk on the subject: How to Be the Best Divorced Guy You Can Be. He admitted that things still felt vertiginous because this person he'd organized his horizon around for so many decades was suddenly absent, which was the deepest mystery of his life so far. Still, a newly anointed high priest of fish-or-cut-bait, he hinted that maybe I too should be thinking along these lines, to which I said, "You're fucking with my resolve."

The only problem now was that he was constantly monitoring himself in new relationships, worried that he was reenacting the same patterns as in his marriage. Was his new girlfriend just an update on his wife? Had his marriage altered him so deeply, at a cellular or microscopic level, that he'd always be looking for the hidden stash, the hidden something, then trying to fix it? Was his girlfriend addicted to overwork or personal chaos, or is it just that we've all got our brands of crazy? But did he want to sign up for this particular brand? Despite having quoted Jung on shadows, I wondered if he now thought that having made a conscious decision to leave a fractured marriage, his relationships hereafter would take place in the bright glare of sunlight.

—

As in so many households across the land, the pandemic had brought certain long-standing patterns to the forefront in mine too, patterns that could also be said to fall under the heading of "substance issues." For instance: why would someone purportedly "on the wagon," and lucky enough to have thus far survived a worldwide extinction event, someone who'd that very day received Dose Number One of the miracle vaccine—as good a sign as any for quite a while that things would finally be *getting better,* a glimmer of hope that "normal life" (however you choose to define it) was just over the horizon—why would that fortunate person choose *that very same day* to fall spectacularly "off the wagon," and drink enough, in an alarmingly short period of time, to effectively *replicate* many of the supremely unpleasant symptoms—nausea, dizziness, chills, brain fog—of the virus he'd thus far managed not to contract? As well as exacerbate whatever nasty short-term side effects the vaccine itself may have produced, aggravated by the fact that being "on the wagon" typically lowers one's levels of alcohol toleration—no one's sicker the next day than a relapsed drunk.

I put the question to my beloved.

I should pause here to note that there are a lot of good reasons people don't write candidly about relationships they're currently in and attempting to sustain (you're obviously not going to write about your sex life—even when it's really great!—if you ever want to have sex with the person again, which leaves a big chunk of coupled reality unsayable), meaning we have few "unvarnished" accounts of what actually transpires in these realms. You don't wish to betray your mate, you don't wish to betray yourself. Tone control is an endemic hazard—the amusing little aside about that cute foible of the mate's turns out to reek of hostility, you'll likely be informed (hopefully before your candid little chronicle hits print), which you somehow failed to notice. The real problem is that you never exactly know what you're really up to when being "candid," because a soulmate lives (by definition) as much or more within the confines of your psyche as having an independent existence "in reality," so you're essentially scribbling in the dark.

Talking about why you drink would be to defeat the purpose of the booze, he responded. Despite the non-answer this was more transparency than I recalled him bringing to previous discussions on the subject. It's not that alcohol enables you to deny whatever reality you're positing, he elaborated. It's that alcohol *is* denial. It's a way of avoiding who you are. That's the whole point—being a drinker means you're skilled at avoiding yourself. You don't want to *be* yourself. You use drinking as a way of finding another self, but that's a stupid way of putting it because obviously there isn't "another" self you can find, he said. You're not Gatsby, you're not on a journey of self-reinvention, you don't have some Platonic conception of yourself, you just don't want to be who you are anymore.

What's wrong with who you are, I asked, pretending for the moment that I too didn't usually want to escape myself and also aware that roughly half the world attempts to control who they are via pharmaceuticals, legally prescribed and otherwise. He said it was an impossible question—sometimes you're fine, other times you think if I don't get out of my skin, if I don't get out of this place I'm in right now . . . Avoiding reality was the only way he'd had any success in life, he pointed out (tenure, fellowships, I suppose he meant, also that he was the only person in his top-tier department who hadn't attended a top-tier grad program, which had left him intellectually scrappy and with a chip on his shoulder about the Ivies). His whole life had been about avoiding what was in front of him. Not that that was sustainable, he admitted, but avoidance means avoiding your own limitations too. The people he'd studied with knew everything. (They were mostly huge alcoholics, of course—here he launched into a story I'd heard before about being at a conference in some podunk college town with a bunch of his intellectual heroes which involved a lot of trips to liquor stores and boozing in hotel rooms.)

Everyone feels like a fraud, I said uncharitably. Go on the internet and read about "imposter complex"—every successful woman has it. Read Simone de Beauvoir: women are obliged to fake their personalities and play at being what they aren't, perpetually on the brink of neurosis. I couldn't summon the same loftiness about self-avoidance he could, to me it was mundane and I didn't feel inclined to rhapsodize about it. I couldn't afford the same romance with my impediments. He had a wonderful ability to make avoidance sound like a creative project, a way of inventing another world. "Take your reality and shove it" was his personal code, which sometimes had its charms. I suppose I have a certain affinity for norm-renegades, while resenting their self-indulgence. A realist's guide to mate selection: the same things that make the person exciting and attractive, an object of your lust, will eventually become the things you wish to chop out of them with a steak knife.

Our differing relations to "avoidance" were a tedious ongoing "issue" between us—my mode is to insist on the reality of things. It's an ethos, an ethos of clear-eyedness; reality-avoiders and glee hounds are (I secretly or not-so-secretly think) fatuous. I'm a critic: I want to see the world clearly. Maybe that overstates it—I just want to have interesting things to say about the world. In service of which I invariably notice what's errant: if there's a dustball in the corner, as there currently was, or a pile of laundry on the bedroom chair (his), I'll notice and most likely comment disparagingly on it. If there's a spot in the vicinity my attention veers immediately to the spot. Maybe hypervigilance is my own response to traumas past, who knows? What I know is that you're probably better off sublimating your traumas into an aesthetic position than trying to booze them away. For him alcohol was a magical elixir that elicits, enhances, and erases emotions all at once. His defense of boozy self-invention had a utopian streak I could admire intellectually but was also laughably romantic, reminiscent of the way he romanticized literary drunks and poetical boozehounds, was prone to tearing up at the plight of the John Berrymans of the world, or pre-pandemic, hanging out with the other neighborhood philosopher-kings, drinking beer on their stoops and talking politics. I liked his openness to the world and those it's kicked around though thought it was less hilarious than he did when he got a ticket from the NYPD for drinking in public (the cop, who was white, screeched to a halt in his squad car and made a point of ticketing the only white guy in the group), while the non-professors had smarts enough to hide their cans in plastic bags.

If the essence of boozing is not facing yourself, it's a repudiation of my clear-eyed ethos. Literally—your eyes get bleary, you put medicinal drops in them called Clear Eyes. In our relationship, I was the medicinal drop. Which I was pretty sick of, sick of being the middle manager, the civilizing force. I don't like cops. I don't like domestic cops, I don't like cultural cops. I've spent decades ranting against both, in and out of print, and here I was, Queen Cop of the homefront. Maybe I'd gotten as addicted to the role as he was to his six-packs. Maybe I was as wedded to trying to fix my mate as my mate was wedded to avoiding a cure. The upside of having a rescue project is at least it saves you from having to rescue yourself, though the Sisyphean element gets oppressive fast if the other party just keeps finding creative new ways to fuck themselves up.

In other words, we'd both managed to choose partners guaranteed to maximally torment us. Each of us was the sort of person guaranteed to drive the other one to drink. I said instructively that reality doesn't care whether you face it or not. Reality doesn't care about your utopianism, reality is going to do what reality is going to do, for instance eat holes in your vital organs, or get you more fucked up from drinking than you used to get because you're not twenty-five anymore, and there are bodily realities that aren't your option to face or reject. If denial enables alcoholism and vice versa, I said, how can two people have a relationship on that basis? (At this point I was boring even myself.)

They can't, he said, but his experience of reality hadn't been pleasant, in fact it had been pretty cruel. I knew this was true, his life had been punctured by loss, including the early loss of a lunatic mother and the paradoxical condition of being left mourning an abuser, which probably explained the propensity for self-punishment. He said he'd learned how to forget things from his mother, in the sense that he could say to his childhood self, "Who cares," when she slapped him around. "It's not a big deal, because she's your mother. She's not punishing *you*. It's not about you," he'd tell himself. He learned from her how to stop keeping accounts (which has upsides and downsides—he's both quick to forgive and feloniously irresponsible). None of this is an explanation or excuse, he said, it's just that reality had trained him to be avoidant. And there the splitting begins: you're telling yourself something that at an emotional level you know can't be true, but you need to believe it anyway.

I myself could sometimes almost feel this monstrous mother's hands around my own throat, dragging me into her unquiet grave too. Her life was a tableau vivant of the mid-century female condition—she might have stepped off the pages of *The Feminine Mystique*, one of those suburban wives Friedan writes about, who simply go berserk one night and run shrieking through the streets without any clothes on. After repeated miscarriages, she'd apparently taken DES, the now-banned anti-miscarriage drug, before it was found to be toxic. She and my boyfriend's older sister, still in her twenties, both died of cancer within a year of each other, his sister's death likely a result of his mother's maternal aspirations—it turned out that DES impacted daughters in the womb, producing high levels of reproductive organ cancers later on. Not that his mother seemed overly fond of the children she managed to successfully deliver, though she did share her love of books with him. (She'd wanted to be an intellectual.) Once she barged into his room while he was reading a porn magazine, which he frantically tried to hide. "It doesn't matter what you read," she said, "you're allowed to bring it into this house." She could be a monster, but she was an open-minded one. Those guilty twin losses were a permanent ice pick in his psyche, a melancholy substratum to his congenital optimism. I guess at some level his mother had been an optimist too.

She died decades before I came on the scene, but at some level her story is now mine as well, given the well-known axiom that men try to turn you (unwittingly or whatever) into their mothers. He's in love with his ghosts, I sometimes think when things aren't going swimmingly between us, but I guess intimacy means being haunted by another person's ghosts in addition to your own. (Sometimes you're also their beneficiary, as with the bibliophilia.) Occasionally when I find myself shrieking like a crazy person, I think—who is this? My family were not shriekers. What god-awful poisonous thing has infected me, hijacked my decorum? The ghost of Mom, apparently. Love perforates us, often way too deeply—as I'd argued to Mason, about the default codependency of normal coupledom.

When Mason suggested that your mate's substance problem gives you a free pass to do what you were going to do anyway, I contemplated that at least having such a mate offers a built-in rationale for whatever free-floating relationship ambivalence one might be bringing to the table. Typically speaking ambivalence is the cardinal relationship sin, maybe even worse than affairs (in practice the two are often linked, as I've chronicled elsewhere). Sadly, it's also the part of yourself you have to renounce, unless you're doing stand-up. (Rodney Dangerfield: "My wife and I were happy for twenty years. Then we met.") We non-comedians are supposed to hide it in the garage where the other person won't find it, though perhaps pledging yourself to a dipsomaniac gives you some wiggle room on this, a useful rationale for clutching your ambivalence tight. *I'm sorry you've got this problem honey, I'm gonna have to keep my emotional distance from you, because we all know how toxic people like you are—I might catch codependency.* (Don't fool yourself, you're going to catch it whatever you do.)

Here too Wilhelm Stekel, the "morally insane" early Freudian, proves helpful. Instead of being either static or stable, we exist in states of permanent oscillation, he wrote, capable of swinging wildly to love and other times wildly to hate. No matter how positive you think you are, the negative always reasserts itself, though for Stekel it's not either/or, it's *both/ and*.

I love reading defenses of ambivalence. I've sometimes thought ambivalence is for me what psoriasis was for John Updike, unlovely but the key to everything, a deformity that becomes a métier. "What was my creativity, my relentless need to produce, but a parody of my skin's embarrassing overproduction?" he speculates. "Was not my thick literary skin, which shrugged off rejection slips and patronizing reviews by the sheaf, a superior version of my poor vulnerable own, and my shamelessness on the page a distraction from my real shame?" It made him a better proofreader, agonizing over typos and factual errors—"the 'spots' on the ideally unflecked text." It gave him a predilection for plots about duplicity and secret lives. It made him fascinated with normalcy—overvaluing it, but also its greatest takedown artist. On this too, I could relate. Transforming your embarrassments into an aesthetic principle and your fugitive emotions into subject matter is at least preferable to foisting them on your intimates, though lacking an aptitude for the "either/or," I prefer both/and.

How to make ambivalence into a creative force in *my* relationship, you ask? I suggest taking up a home improvement project, namely the project of changing your beloved into the person they really *should* be, a project that lockdown conditions left loads of time for. What month was it that I proposed a behavioral modification regime designed to turn my boyfriend into a "mindful" drinker, one who'd measure out two responsible ounces of wine for cocktail hour, and another four upstanding ounces with dinner. One (largish) glass of wine a day total seemed an acceptable limit to a beneficent behaviorist such as myself. He went along with the new regime good-naturedly (until he didn't). Mason had mentioned that Russian doctors treat alcoholism by getting alcoholics drunk on boilermakers multiple days in a row, then giving them nausea drugs. I joked about trying that in my own household. "Which speaks to a sort of desperation," he pointed out. Or a worrisome affinity for the lab coat, I thought. One motive for trying to fix your mate is obviously the anxiety that their degree of fucked-upness is a metric of your own bad judgment in the eyes of the world (in truth no one's looking, they have their own problems). Another friend's boyfriend is a psychiatrist who happens to work with drunks and substance abusers. We had a social Zoom with them around this time and I asked what he thought of the behavior modification plan. He said a lot of things I didn't understand about GABA receptors, cortisol, the conflicts between the forebrain and the limbic system (the lizard brain, he helpfully addended), then pronounced gnomically, "Once you're a pickle, you'll never go back to being a cucumber."

Recently I streamed the big European movie import of the year, *Another Round,* nominated for all sorts of awards, about a bunch of Danish high school teachers who decide—having read some crackpot article by a Norwegian psychiatrist named Finn Skårderud which claims we're all born with blood alcohol levels that are *too low*—to drink constantly every day to maintain a blood alcohol level of 0.05 percent. Studies have supposedly shown that creativity is boosted when you're buzzed, if you keep yourself just under the legal limit. The main idiot (I mean protagonist), Martin, happens, like my partner, to teach history, though Martin is indifferent about it and a depressed sad sack generally. He lacks self-confidence and *joie de vivre;* he worries that he's boring and his marriage is indeed DOA, though his wife struck me as admirably patient and attractive.

Then he and his pals start day-drinking and the results are astounding. They're transformed! Suddenly their students love them, they're charming, magnanimous, creative, energized. Their posture improves, they dress better, Martin is suddenly handsome. No longer a schlump, he takes the family kayaking; he and his wife get it on again. Aside from minor mishaps like running nose-first into a door at school, everything's great. Except that the rules of the new regime—no drinking after eight p.m., breathalyze yourself frequently, and don't go above 0.05 percent—soon go out the window. "I haven't felt this good in years," says one of the crew. "What about getting higher?" Why not push it to 0.08 percent? Why not 0.10 percent? They're not alcoholics, because *they're* deciding when to drink. Except soon they're drinking all the time and experimenting with absinthe cocktails to get maximally drunk. One guy's wife leaves him after he stumbles home drunk and pees the bed. Martin wakes up in the street bleeding with the neighbors standing around pointing, his kid has to haul him inside. His marriage too is done. Three of the friends give up the experiment and swear off booze; the fourth—Tommy, the gym teacher—shows up at a faculty meeting devoted to discussing the recent problem of staff drinking on the job (empties keep being found in the storeroom) visibly plastered out of his gourd. The end for him isn't pretty.

Watching a bunch of middle-aged men sitting around drinking themselves into incomprehension was, I found, excruciating. Needless to say, it's left to Martin's wife to repair the marriage—miraculously (or inexplicably) she texts him in the penultimate scene, just as he and the pals are commemorating Tommy's death with a round of drinks, saying she wants to reunite. Martin, apparently in a former life a jazz dancer, does an exuberant dance-parkour number surrounded by drunken revelers and joyously flings himself into the harbor. We freeze mid-jeté on what looks like a grand leap of freedom, but is actually—to a clear-eyed observer such as myself—a perilous dive into the drink.

Like a self-pitying middle-aged male drunk, this movie wants it all ways. Sure boozing can kill you and estrange your family, but you can dance like no one's watching—in other words, the movie's as schizoid as being married to an alcoholic who's lovely and caring one moment, raging the next. It demands you take its dumb premise seriously, like someone who's imbibed too much laboriously explaining something to you at a dinner party. It thinks it's funnier than it is, sometimes known as self-indulgence. I was surprised at the degree of my antipathy to these frivolities. Did I mention the part about pissing the bed? Maybe alcohol feigns a path to escape, but one that traps you (and your partner, unless or until they decamp) in the deadness of a repetition compulsion.

But listen to me getting all self-righteous! Like Martin's wife. No doubt she too resented being cast in the role of abstinence officer, killjoy, the death of the party. It turns out she's been having an affair, which Martin never suspected. As with my friend Mason and probably the rest of the coupled world, we keep ledgers and want the recompenses we're owed.

Regarding his own recent fall from the wagon, my boyfriend explained, "Someday we're all going to die whatever we do," adopting an irritatingly nihilistic philosophical mode. I suppose it was pandemic-speak: we were trying to save ourselves from a deadly virus while knowing (and denying) that each day brings us closer to an inevitable demise no matter what we do. Was wanting to numb a little bit of pain along the way such an irrational response? I was having a harder time than usual summoning the trusty wagging finger.

My boyfriend reminded me of a talk we'd watched online the week before by Lewis Hyde, whose new book was all about forgetting (*A Primer for Forgetting: Getting Past the Past*). Hyde spoke about the way oral cultures were able to keep their equilibrium by sloughing off memories that didn't help them cope with the present, whereas in print and digital culture memories can never truly disappear. Either you learn to forget the past or you're stranded in it. It happens that my boyfriend has the kind of near-photographic memory that lets him forget nothing—anything that's ever happened to him might have happened yesterday. Nothing recedes, even page numbers are stuck there forever, like Dustin Hoffman in *Rain Man* (as I like to taunt him because I'm someone who remembers nothing). Trying to heal the lacerations of the past by swimming into oceans of alcohol is even more futile in his case than it is for people with neurotypical style memories, he keeps washing up to shore with the same sharp-focus pain. Hyde's book was about how these places of non-forgetting become entrenched forms of melancholy. If you can't slough off the memories you need to forget, you're sentenced to repress them, mutilate them—and, of course, endlessly relive them.

Hyde quotes Adam Phillips: "People come for psychoanalytic treatment because they are remembering in a way that does not free them to forget." They're remembering by way of their symptoms, Hyde glosses. But there's something hopeful in there too, he proposes: the compulsion to repeat is "a kind of stuttering toward speech." That's what alcohol does too, said my boyfriend. It conjures your emotions and quells them, it incites your emotions and suffocates them. The problem is you keep reliving the past, then obviously you keep drinking more so as not to, and then the cycle starts again. The problem with *not* drinking is that you feel like you're constantly in the middle of a fire drill. You have to block all the impulses coming from within you, you have to distrust yourself. It builds up this paranoic edge against the world, you're in this state of constant self-surveillance. All your demons are milling around watching you, and you're watching them, and you have to guard against yourself and them at every minute.

I was both grateful for and unsettled by this conversation, but a lot of pandemic conversations felt that way—people were summing up their lives and their regrets, and nothing about that was casual. Yeah, I said, but what if one person's escape strategy or solace is the other person's heartbreak? I was admiring his eloquence while wondering cynically if people are the most prevaricating when they seem the most disclosing. I suppose cynicism is a (temporary) inoculation against disappointment. I asked if he'd read the email I'd sent a few days before (Subject: "Lines, where to draw?"), with a link to something I'd seen online, a query originally posted on Reddit's relationship advice forum, from a woman complaining about her boyfriend's sleeping habits. It had struck me as a parable of something, though I wasn't sure precisely what.

The two had been dating for three years though she hadn't until recently actually seen his apartment. When she did she was stunned to see there was no bed in the bedroom, instead there was a huge pile of clothes and towels in the middle of the room, which he referred to as his "nest." He kind of curled himself into a ball in the middle, and piled some clothes and towels on top of himself. That's how he slept. It emerged that he hadn't previously had her over because he was embarrassed about the nest. He was okay with her sleeping on the couch if she wanted. She really liked him so she tried sleeping in the nest with him, but it was uncomfortable and weird, also it smelled, so she eventually went to sleep in the living room. In the morning he accused her of hating his nest and got defensive about it, saying that if they were going to take the next step and move in together, she'd need to accept his nest. She said if they moved in together they were getting a bed. (Also he didn't *wash* the clothes pile since he argued he wasn't wearing them, they were just "nesting materials," which she additionally objected to.) In any case, they weren't currently speaking, though she was wondering whether a two-bedroom place might be the solution.

People on the forum were unusually engaged by this dilemma, with responses roughly split between compassion and revulsion. Some were adamant that the nest simply crossed the line (invisible but always hovering) of social norms—break up immediately if you have any respect for yourself, they insisted. He isn't going to change, ditch him now. Others leaped in with practical suggestions and compromises— maybe a beanbag chair? Couldn't he just wash the clothes? Relativists pointed out that this was no less weird than furries (people who dress up in animal costumes with human characteristics and consort with others similarly dressed). A cross-culturalist said Pacific Islanders sleep in nests. Split between compassion and revulsion myself, I kept thinking about the situation. Where *do* you draw the line, when you're congenitally drawn to norm-challengers?

You could tell right away which of the respondents were good codependency candidates—these were the (like me) flexible thinkers, the ones who said things like "If he's otherwise great, often 'red flags' can be worked through." The social-worker types who wanted to know if there was trauma in the nester's past—maybe he came from an underprivileged situation? They wanted to get to the root of the problem, to nurture and understand him, adapt themselves to his needs. "Find out what about the nest appeals to him," someone suggested, "and see what you can do to replicate those feelings." Or "If you want to pursue this relationship, suggest compromises and let him know that you're not judging him." They were so deeply involved in the nester's problems their autonomy was already sailing out the window. They were adaptable to a fault! They connected (even thirdhand) to the shame the nester must have felt. They knew he'd been hiding such a big part of himself and were moved that he was finally trying to be open.

Someone on the forum suggested that the nester and his girlfriend try to build a nest together, one that suited both of them. "One not built out of clothes, and that is hygienic." Yes, I thought. Something in the suggestion made me a little teary. Yes, isn't this what we're all trying to do, in our feeble and defended ways? Just build a nest together, for whatever short time we have?

Another part of me rebelled. Get a grip, I chided myself. How much weird self-solacing (and by the way, who *isn't* damaged?) should another person be expected to tolerate for the sake of a relationship? Then a third voice chimed in: What if your standards are so rigid and uncompassionate that no one but an anal compulsive with thousand-dollar sheets from Frette can possibly meet them?

I've always been amused by the opening of anthropologist Mary Douglas's classic study *Purity and Danger,* which brilliantly dismantles the stability of our concepts of dirt and cleanliness, famously redescribing dirt as "matter out of place" (dirt in a flowerbed isn't dirty, shoes on the bed are). She begins with a wry acknowledgment to her husband, crediting him with being a source of inspiration for the book since "In matters of cleanliness his threshold of tolerance is so much lower than my own that he more than anyone else has forced me into taking a stand on the relativity of dirt." I imagine her trying to make the case to her obviously more fastidious spouse and wonder if the cleaning arguments ever drove either of them to drink. (She *was* a lifelong Catholic.) I suspect Douglas would have little time for the prescriptions of today's codependency gurus about maintaining "healthy boundaries" in your relationships.

What you learn from Douglas is that there are no boundaries without anxiety and defensiveness; they produce as much distress as they alleviate. The joke's on us. Other people are a contagion no matter how hard you try to establish your autonomy ("pollution avoidance" in her lexicon)—"The colonization of each other's minds is the price we pay for thought," she tartly observes.

Doubtless the price we pay for intimacy too. Reflecting on my own love life, I'm sometimes reminded of Charlie Citrine's reflection about his impossible girlfriend Renata in Bellow's novel *Humboldt's Gift*—"for an atypical foot you need an atypical shoe. If in addition to being atypical you are fastidious—well, you have your work cut out for you." She's the shoe, he's the foot. (In my reflections I'm the foot.) And is there any typical foot, Citrine/Bellow wonders, concluding (if a little rhapsodically for a Chicagoan, my own hometown too) that "love is a power that can't let us alone. It can't because we owe our existence to acts of love performed before us, because love is a standing debt of the soul."

Love as a debt collector sounds right—charging usurious rates, kneecapping you if you resist.

4

LOVE AND CHAOS

COVID introduced new challenges and wrinkles for any-one who still cares about the antiquated concept of privacy: among them, "contact tracing." You can see why some might be resistant—married folk conducting clandestine affairs, to pick a random example. No surprise, it turned out that the demographic least opposed to sharing their locations and medical data with whatever entity requested them were mil-lennials, who live much of their lives in public anyway, includ-ing their love lives.

As was brought home to me when my former student Zelda and I started Zooming every week or two during the early COVID months, at first just to catch up, then because I became vicariously fascinated by her swashbuckling stories of love under lockdown and the characters who peopled her world, tales she spun expertly (she'd studied narrative with me, after all), always leaving enough dangling threads that I started comparing her to Scheherazade of "The Thousand and One Nights," not knowing if she knew the reference. (I only remembered later what a rapey little tale it is, something

that hadn't occurred to me when I'd first read it as a child.)
Many of her references eluded me also, Zelda being queer,
Black, and very online, and me being none of those things,
though we seemed to connect on other planes—she's irreverent about pieties and intellectualizes her feelings in ways that
seem painfully familiar to me, also wryly observant about
relationship follies. Having grown up navigating around
neurotically exasperating parents she doesn't expect a lot of
hand-holding from the world, just carves out her own tra-
jectories, which was another reason we got along. (I'm not
much of a hand-holder.) We'd seen each other occasionally
in the years since she'd graduated, but Zooming from our
bedrooms and living rooms amplified the intimacy more than
sitting across a table at Starbucks had in our former lives,
one of those incongruous but welcome old/new connections
facilitated by social desperation and technological proximity.

Given how stultified my own life felt, I was definitely up
for hearing about how people who are young, lonely, and
horny were coping under the new restrictions. Zelda and
her friends—queer and straight, fluid or experimenting,
various races and backgrounds—were united by one thing:
having grown up with the internet they were, I soon realized, creative geniuses at using their phones and screens to
create unbelievable romantic chaos and misery, which they
apparently thrived on because no one was exactly giving it
up, even as a pandemic raged. The chaos was contagious, or
to deploy a more timely idiom, *viral*. Everyone was highly

skilled at deploying all available digital means—social media, screenshots, texts and DMs, pseudonymity, online exposé and shaming—to stir up emotional drama, or inflict and sustain injury. There was constant romantic intrigue and espionage—Zelda referred to info gleaned online as "intel," and regarded herself as an expert in the dark art of cross-platform research. She felt there was basically nothing you couldn't find out about someone by comparing their posts across different social media sites, which sounded both gratifying and incredibly time-consuming.

While the everyone's-a-click-away element of online life generated newfangled versions of interpersonal mischief and triangulation, in other respects her world could be alarmingly traditional. The community's moral judgments rained down on transgressors; there were virtual stockades and mandated exile. It was village life reprised, replete with the usual scolds and busybodies, like *Middlemarch* but with more hooking up. The appetite for relational turmoil seemed insatiable—jealousy, betrayals, accusation, and confrontation—especially now that everyone was bored and there was little else to do but stir pots and see who got scalded. Which could be fun, though there was inevitable spillover into real life, which could be less fun. There was often no little self-deception involved, I noticed: people posting things online yet also expecting privacy; getting upset when strangers knew things about them, things they had themselves propelled into the world. In any case, it was accepted that your private business played out in public because that's just how things are.

Of course it's increasingly how things are for all of us, which was among the reasons Zelda's stories riveted me: what used to be known as the public/private divide has pretty much vanished no matter what generation you are. To be sure, the distinction itself didn't exist before what we call modernity, and maybe the big story of the twenty-first century will be how it was once again jettisoned—between the post-9/11 surveillance state and the stepped-up monetization of inner life known as digital capitalism, privacy is little more than a fading memory. Zelda and her friends just took the compulsory disclosure a few steps further, refashioning it into emotionally messy performance art and collective entertainment.

She and her crowd were creative types—writers, filmmakers, rappers, YouTubers—mostly underemployed, minus health insurance, politically aware and deeply jaded. Especially after the outcome of the 2020 election—was that all George Floyd's death had meant? Biden? Most of them were saddled with crippling student debt, meaning they couldn't imagine much of a future; those inclined to procreate couldn't even begin to think about kids. The labor market had broken down even before COVID—what would await when things reopened? Economists were saying the pandemic would produce a "lost generation"—the share of national wealth owned by millennials was already only a quarter of what boomers owned at the same age, and down from where Gen X had been too.

Everyone was trapped in a *Groundhog Day* of annoying roommates, cheap apartments, and freelancing, wondering when they were going to reach adulthood. Their love lives had a lot in common with the gig economy—fast turnover and capricious conditions. With the pandemic, people were even more depressed and stuck in place—a high percentage were on antidepressants or anxiety meds with predictable consequences. When I asked Zelda if it messed up people's sex lives she mentioned a previous girlfriend who'd been on Lexapro and couldn't have orgasms. I'd read about millennials having less sex than previous post–sexual revolution generations, but Zelda at least was having plenty (and could be pretty amusing on the subject).

Even at the height of the quarantine her first dates mostly ended up in bed, as people were doing a lot of drinking and molly out of boredom and feeling unrooted, so sex naturally followed. After some interrogation and a few perfunctory negotiations—had you been tested? how many people are you seeing?—the social distancing got more proximate, the masks came off, and bedrooms beckoned. Compared to the general state of sexual lament I'd been hearing and reading about from other singles, Zelda just treated pandemic dating as a practical problem to be solved: she'd meet someone online and invite them over for a wine tasting, a bit of *Playboy*-era suavity that cracked me up. The romantic pragmatism ran in the family—one of her relatives was currently dating her weed guy, a two-birds-one-stone approach to provisioning that I admired for its efficiency. Zelda does think queers tend to be more direct about what they want, and that women dating women are more likely to have sex sooner than straight women, who are less comfortable having strange men to their places.

Zelda was happy to share her intel with me and I liked hearing it, though she did occasionally describe herself as an "oversharer," something she said she had to "work on." (I asked her not to work on it quite yet, as she'd said she was very open to being a character in a story I would write and was giving me creative license, as long as she got a cool pseudonym.) But oversharing is obviously sutured into digital life, its *sine qua non*—she knew the internet totally extracts it from you and it's not exactly in the realm of free choice. Erich Fromm (who came up earlier in the role of Karen Horney's truculent lover) is helpful on these relays between history and subjectivity: "In order for a society to function, its members must acquire the kind of character which makes them *want* to act in the ways they *have* to act as members of that society." Which is slightly depressing.

To update Fromm: if we're compelled at this point in history to continuously externalize our most private selves and all the most popular new technologies and genres, from social media to reality TV, are devoted to fostering the project (while strip-mining your inner life for profit), clearly this is the form of subjectivity required of us at this stage in the development of capitalism. Early capitalism piggybacked on the Protestant

Ethic, sucking up happy-go-lucky peasants and churning out industrious wage slaves. Digital capitalism wants your data, not your labor, a renewable resource to exploit and profit from by refashioning us all into industrious oversharers.

Zelda would occasionally try to set limits on the sharing, but no one around her had any which made that tough. I noticed she could talk about the most painful things that had happened in her life with great ease, she wasn't boundaried and imploded in the way I felt myself to be. Who knows, maybe the compulsory spillage has some ancillary psychological benefits, but the point is that you can barely participate in the economy *without* being an oversharer. Even those fucking security questions—"What was the name of your first pet?" If you don't want to have to walk to the bank to deposit a check you're going to have to empty your soul into the little box, reliving the painful death of Apples over and over on command until it's no longer your memory, it's theirs.

Everything must be disclosed, nothing kept "in." But if every passing flicker of sensory perception is immediately posted, shared, and subjected to the scrutiny of the collectivity, maybe "inner life" is itself now a passé conceit. I wondered if Zelda and her circle had turned online emotional display into a kind of erotics, like those who fetishize car accidents in J. G. Ballard's *Crash,* "a new sexuality, born from a perverse technology." Erotics aside, all that externalizing could get pretty exhausting, like a full-time job, and it's not like it helped pay the rent.

Though she'd always struck me as a low-drama sort, Zelda turned out to be at the center of an astounding amount of romantic uproar in the sagas she related. Maybe it's the fate of the stoical, those who handle their emotions too adeptly, to attract drama queens and hysterics, becoming a magnet for lovers with multiple grievances who suffer life's injuries most extravagantly (or maybe I'm overidentifying). I'd open a conversation by casually asking what was new and Zelda would say "Everything's pretty chill," then suddenly recall that actually there'd been a big blowup the week before when her new girlfriend Olivia, with whom things were going really great because she was a super-calm person, had posted photos of the two of them on Twitter, which Zelda retweeted, which is where a previous girlfriend, Camille, whom Zelda had briefly dated around a month before, spotted them. Zelda and Camille had really only hung out a few times, and things hadn't really clicked so they'd eventually just stopped talking, but in a pretty organic way, or so Zelda thought. She hadn't *ghosted* her but they weren't really vibing, and Camille sort of said the same thing, so Zelda felt like it was super-mutual. That is, until Camille responded to her retweet of Olivia's photos with *"lol wow."* (I was scribbling notes to keep up with the cast of characters.)

Camille and Olivia have a lot of mutual followers—as mentioned, village life updated—and some of Zelda's friends favorited Camille's tweet, mistakenly thinking Camille was *happy* for Zelda, though Zelda knew that wasn't what she'd meant. Zelda tweeted back a *"?"* to Camille, meaning "I am confused." Like why was Camille being edgy about the photos? When Camille didn't answer, Zelda tried a different line of communication, texting *"Hey, I saw your tweets and what's up?"*

In the meantime, Zelda's friend Frank texted Zelda some tweets of Camille's from earlier that day, tweets that Camille had already deleted, saying, *"God, I wish people would be transparent when they're dating and just say they've met someone else, not that they're 'bad at communication' and like lol, women are just as bad as men are."* This was, Zelda explained to me (I'm not on Twitter much and needed remedial assistance), what is known as a *subtweet*, meaning a tweet that doesn't directly mention anyone's name but is clearly *aimed* at someone, and that someone, in this case, was Zelda. As Frank discerned, for reasons that would soon be revealed.

So Zelda texted Camille again, this time to assure her that even though it might *seem* fast for them to be posting photos of each other, Olivia and she had really just met. Camille finally texted back *"lol Zelda,"* which was another thing Zelda hadn't liked about her, that there was an *"lol"* attached to every text. "You're not laughing and I'm not either, so like, stop it," Zelda said (to me) with more than usual asperity. Camille was not appeased. Doubling down, she texted back, *"Lol Zelda, the math is not right, and how does that make sense, we just stopped talking four weeks ago, so how are you in a relationship already? You had to be dating her when you were dating me.*"

I was struggling to keep up with the emotional logic, which struck me as exotic. As far as normative relationship protocols, Zelda's was a world theoretically adjacent to mine—contemporaneous, Anglophone, bipedal—but it was an entirely different emotional enterprise, more like competitive tango or irregular warfare than what I was accustomed to, where "playing it cool" (at least at the beginning) was regarded as desire-inducing, and what one strived to achieve, if sometimes with difficulty. There must be vastly higher expectations of one another in these milieus, I surmised, or maybe an excess of romantic confidence, if someone felt comfortable issuing recriminations a month after a casual thing. Camille had never even spent the night at Zelda's place, at least according to Zelda, who speculated that maybe Camille had liked her more than she'd thought at the time, which was awkward. Or did pandemic dating lead people to expect commitment sooner? Either way, if they get bent out of shape because a casual thing turned out to be short-lived, this was surely the formula for much interpersonal angst, especially given the incessant online scrolling and monitoring of exes, which was systematic and went deep. Everyone was pretty much running their own in-house cyberintelligence operation in addition to whatever paying jobs they held, at-will employees in their own digital sweatshops.

Zelda was trying to explain to Camille that she hadn't

cheated on her when her text message bubble turned green, meaning Camille had *blocked* her, which seemed harsh, I remarked, prompting from Zelda another remedial digression on the semiotics of blocking. I'd always thought messages being green just meant the other person wasn't using iMessage, which Zelda confirmed, but if they'd *been* blue previously, *then* turned green, you knew you were blocked. And if the bubble never returned to being blue—Zelda here paused to check her phone, yup still green—that means you're still blocked. Whereas when another of her exes, Heather, blocks her, as she periodically does, the bubble goes green, then blue again when Heather relents and unblocks her.

Blocking and unblocking texts, along with the monitoring and indicting of exes was, I was learning, another ongoing form of interpersonal drama. Zelda checked her Instagram, yes Camille had blocked her there too, though possibly this was a *"soft block,"* an especially devious form of online interpersonal warfare, accomplished by first blocking the person then unblocking them, meaning that when they next go to your Insta page they discover they're not following you anymore, and understand they're being shunned. Zelda was continuing to check her various accounts while we spoke. "Oh, that's weird, she didn't block me on Twitter, but she blocked my text messages," she noted with bemusement. Zelda inferred that Camille's not blocking her on Twitter meant "I still want you to see when I post something about you." I was thrilled to be getting a real-time glimpse of this generational emotional style: masterly indirection, relationships conducted by means of brazen passive-aggression and unstated expectations, according to which violators could be publicly punished, including for crimes they didn't know they'd committed. Additionally, blocking someone didn't end things, it was a method for keeping them churning.

Zelda seemed to know a surprising amount about being blocked, I said bemusedly. She'd always struck me as such a level person, what accounted for people being so *upset* with her all the time? She said people rarely block you because they genuinely don't want you to get in contact, most of the time it's a bit of performance, like: "I need you to know that I'm upset." Another girlfriend, Sabina, would block her when she was pissed off about something, then *tell* Zelda she was blocked, then *text* to let her know that if Zelda needed to get in touch here was her best friend's phone number. This was one of the reasons I liked talking to Zelda, she saw life as a comedy of manners, though she also confessed she was worried she might be a love addict and was handling her emotions in non-healthful ways. I said I thought she was just in an experimental phase of life.

Also, isn't that what these platforms want from us, to imbricate themselves in our emotional lives? This is, to be sure, the history of technological innovation in a nutshell: the successive refashioning of our psyches into welcome mats for the latest thing, from the printing press to the telephone. Consider the post-medieval architectural innovation known as the hallway—finally you didn't have to barge through someone's bedroom to get to the next room, or they through yours. Everyone got used to having sex behind closed doors, which came to be the norm—and what enormous consequences for psychological life that must have incurred! Now the hallways were being torn down and the bedroom doors flung open again. As our psychologies adjust to the hegemony of the internet and its overlords' designs for us, it will eventually just feel like "who we are."

But back to Frank—why had he screenshotted Camille's texts? What was up with him? Zelda explained that Frank, a rapper with various day jobs, and she had known each other since college, talked about everything all the time, and knew a lot of the same people. I'd been imagining him as one of those mischief-making characters in an Iris Murdoch novel, the type who likes disrupting people's relationships, chortling from the sidelines. She protested that he was super-sweet and always looking out for her, though okay, the screenshots were definitely a bit of drama-instigation.

So why *had* he sent her Camille's tweets? "Okay, this is kind of messy," she said, laughing a little self-consciously. Zelda had known that Frank knew Camille—in fact she'd first encountered Camille on one of Frank's social media pages, and texted him when she and Camille first started dating to say "*Wow, Camille's cute and kind of cool.*" Frank hadn't at first told Zelda that he'd also had a brief thing with Camille until Zelda said, "You're acting weird, like did you sleep with her," and he said yeah, and Zelda was like, okay whatever. Frank *also* knew Olivia, Zelda's current girlfriend, and he was just scrolling through his timeline and saw Camille's tweets, figured they were about Zelda and probably thought, Camille's making a fool of herself, so I'm gonna screenshot those tweets because they'll be gone soon.

Frank hadn't wanted to say anything negative about Camille while Zelda was into her, though eventually Zelda started thinking on her own that Camille was kind of stiff and uncommunicative, and Frank finally informed her, "Yeah, Camille was always pretty weird." When Zelda sent him Camille's response to her tweet of the photos of her and Olivia, asking "What does *'lol, wow'* mean?" Frank was like, "Oh, you didn't see what she said yesterday," and passed on the now deleted tweets to Zelda.

"What's the deal with screenshotting?" I asked. "Do you just assume everybody's going to delete everything they post so you need a copy of it?" It turns out there's quite an art to this practice among social media savants. You especially want to screenshot subtweets, Zelda explained, because the deliberate *omission* of someone's name signals it could be something potentially *embarrassing,* which is basically what you're after. Did Zelda screenshot regularly? No, not really, she said, just funny stuff. Or controversial stuff, like if someone tweets something kind of crazy, she'd definitely screenshot that. (In other words, she was screenshotting constantly.) She'd never really thought about the process or the instincts required to do it successfully, but probably everyone who's grown up on the internet just sort of intuits *"Oh, this is a really bad tweet, this is gonna be bad."* You feel embarrassed for the person and know they're going to delete it, so you screenshot it. It was essentially another non-paying job, I gathered; they were archivists of embarrassment, always looking for the goods ("the receipts") on each other to file away for possible future deployment.

I'd previously known about (and had my own run-ins with) the millennial prosecutorial spirit on campus,* and it can't be ignored that the takedown mode is this generation's forté. The Camille situation was additionally incestuous because Camille hadn't known that Zelda knew that Camille had slept with Frank, and she'd get really weird when Zelda brought him up. Zelda admitted to deriving a bit of glee about having intel on Camille that Camille didn't know about, but Camille also didn't seem like someone who could take the embarrassment had Zelda revealed what she knew, so it felt okay to conceal it. (She tried to think ethically about her deceptions, I gathered.) I asked if Camille had realized that Frank was the one who'd screenshotted the tweets she'd deleted and passed them to Zelda. Zelda didn't think so—they have a lot of mutual followers and friends, so anyone could have been the culprit.

I still saw Frank as a Murdochian figure, the mischie-

---

* The subject of my last book.

vous trickster. What else does Frank get up to, I queried, wanting more novelistic details. Does he have a girlfriend? I learned that his last girlfriend had really hated Zelda for some reason—never wanted to hang out with Zelda and Frank when they went out, yet was supremely miffed when they went somewhere without her. Zelda was like, "Girl I do not want him, what is the problem here?" Following the principle that whatever people deny about sex is invariably true, I asked if she *had* ever wanted Frank. Well, they'd had sex once maybe seven years ago, but it was pretty weird, and they were both like, "Hmm, let me see . . . Um, no." It also turned out that Frank's girlfriend had herself been in a "questioning" mode for a while, constantly telling Frank that she—the girlfriend—was queer and wanted to date women. Frank thought they were supposed to be monogamous, but he also wanted her to have her freedom. Was that why the girlfriend had an issue with Zelda—did Zelda signify queerness and the girlfriend was uncomfortable with her own? This was Zelda's surmise.

And what *had* Camille been after when she'd posted tweets implying Zelda had been cheating on her—was this business of calling people out for their sexual ethics (even absent an agreement that the two were in an actual relationship) part of the #MeToo aftermath? Zelda thought yes, it had definitely been an attempted takedown, but a failed one, which was why Camille deleted the tweets. People hadn't even known they'd dated so no one cared about Camille's accusations.

At the same time, there was definitely a glut of "I'm gonna cancel you" and "I'm gonna hold you accountable" in these circles, which Zelda herself was against. They were all supposed to be big prison abolitionists and restorative justice types, but when they got on the internet it was like shame shame, punishment punishment—*"I'm going to humble you, I'm going to show the people what you did."* Her view, which I more than shared, was that people have to let go of the cops in their heads, but a lot of her friends weren't just cops, they were executioners—they literally wanted to make people suffer, which she found despicable. She'd unfollowed people she otherwise admired because they were so fixated on punishing everyone, especially over perceived minor sexual transgressions. The new thing was responding to someone's tweet with the phrase "Is this you?" and pulling up some years-old out-of-context tweet that contradicted whatever piety the person was now asserting. I asked if she ever worried this could happen to her, and she said that anyone with a brain had already gone back and deleted every past tweet with any incriminating searchable phrase.

Why such interest in conflict production, other than that we're living through the worst time ever and millennials in many ways have it toughest? I was curious about the demographic of these would-be punishers: who was most invested in the takedown mode—was it women? activists? queers?

Zelda thought queers were definitely doing a lot of it, and was philosophical about the etiology: there's obviously a bitterness to being discriminated against and feeling like you're unwanted, which translates into a fixation with putting people in their place. There were just a lot of very *bitter* people on the internet, she diagnosed, eager to mess up people's livelihoods or generate actual death threats.

What about the boomerang effect, I asked, meaning doesn't what goes around come around? I've always thought (and experienced) that whatever aggression you put out into the world eventually returns to smack you in the face. Weren't people worried about their incendiary tweets coming up in job interviews and derailing their future careers? Zelda said sure, the anxiety was out there, but less for Black people. There was a running joke on Black Twitter, she said, laughing: "Something just happened to me, I'm headed to H.R." It was white men who were losing their jobs, and Black people, Black Twitter, facilitating it—"Karens call the manager. Black Twitter calls your job." I said I supposed anti-semitism probably still comes back at people, or anti-gay stuff—I was recalling Kevin Hart having to step down from hosting the Oscars. (A few months after our conversation a youngish Black woman editor also had to resign from *Teen Vogue* because of homophobic and anti-Asian tweets back in high school.) Zelda agreed, mentioning a TV host who'd had his show taken away because of anti-semitic conspiracy theories. I briefly wondered if we were in dicey territory, me her

Jewish-Karen former professor, she a Black Twitter habitué, and I was aware that there were certain things, for all the conversational frankness, that we probably couldn't easily talk about.

Meanwhile Zelda was having a lot of feelings for Olivia, which made the world seem slightly better, though she also knew about herself that she got involved with people way too quickly and fell in love every other week. She and Olivia sat around on Friday nights watching *The Great British Bake Off* and just chilling, and obviously she wanted the pandemic to end, but in the meantime they were embarking on huge jigsaw puzzles together and having the time of their lives, though Olivia's social media posts were also generating a certain level of emotional mess, with Zelda as chief foreman on the cleanup crew, yet another unpaid gig.

I requested details and learned that a few weeks earlier, Tania, who was one of Zelda's ex-girlfriend Heather's best friends, had contacted Olivia out of the blue—well not quite out of the blue, this was after Olivia posted photos of Zelda on "Finsta"—requesting to talk to Olivia on the phone about something. I was finding it challenging to follow this new set of connections, and also what the hell was "Finsta"?

So there's Instagram where you do your regular posting, Zelda informed me, then there's Finsta, which is short for Fake Instagram, where people make *fake* profiles, meaning you don't use your own photo on the avatars, or your own name. Finsta is where you post your most "private" thoughts and photos, or screenshots of text message threads with people that you want to complain about. Finsta is where you talk about sex and who you're dating, kind of like a diary you keep in public, and since it's a private account the only people following you are people who are supposedly super-close to you. It's like "word vomit," but since it's on the "story" feature of Instagram whatever you post only stays up for twenty-four hours.

Zelda's Finsta has around twenty followers, and she doesn't know how many Olivia has because they're not on each other's Finstas, and Zelda's scruples about it are that she'd never ask what Olivia posted, though she could surreptitiously find out if she wanted to, as they have many shared friends. "So you're talking about how sex is with your new girlfriend with twenty people?" I asked. She laughed. Finsta was definitely a recipe for chaos, she said, and a lot of people just use it to get their fix of that.

Zelda had sort of known when she and Olivia got together that there'd be trouble—researching Olivia's followers (as she habitually did when she liked someone, while chastising herself for the compulsion to do it) she'd observed that Tania (Heather's friend) was "liking" a lot of Olivia's posts, and with Olivia now assiduously tweeting and Finsta-posting about them, there was obviously little Tania didn't know about the relationship or presumably pass on to Heather, who was, by Zelda's account, something of an emotional terrorist. Indeed, the day after Olivia's last Finsta post about them,

Heather called Zelda having a total meltdown, crying and saying she'd thought they were going to get back together. Zelda didn't know what to say—it had been a year since they'd split up! Heather wanted to know if the sex was better with Olivia and other crazy stuff, and Zelda was saying, Heather, we shouldn't be having this conversation. She asked how Heather had known about Olivia and Heather said, "I can literally tell you when you all went on your first date!"

Heather and Zelda had first started following each other on Twitter after a mutual friend pointed out that they were both angry and weird in the same way, and soon they'd become super-close, meeting at coffee shops to trade work and talk about their love lives. This went on for three years, then Heather moved away and they were in less touch. At one point she came back for a visit, Zelda had just broken up with someone, and Heather just said out of the blue, "Do you want to have sex, because I haven't had sex in a while." Zelda was like sure, even though there'd never really been any sexual vibe between them, not even flirting.

The problem was that then Heather wanted to text and FaceTime for six hours a day, which made things intense very fast, and not in the healthiest way. Heather came back a few weeks later and stayed with Zelda for two weeks, which was Zelda's first taste of Heather wanting literally *all her attention*. Heather would blow off her other friends or not tell them she was in town, she just wanted to stay home with Zelda, which was romantic for a few days, but for Zelda it wasn't a staycation, she had to work to pay her bills. Heather kept wanting Zelda to call off her shift (Zelda was bartending) because she didn't want to be alone for six or seven hours, and Zelda started feeling pretty codependent too, and let Heather derail her life when she came to town, which started being more often, like every month for a week at a time.

During their friendship period Heather had cried about her ex-boyfriend and their codependence. Zelda thought it sounded really unhealthy, then went and got in the same situation, which she later berated herself for. There were other areas of tension, like finances. Heather was constantly losing things because she never carried a wallet—one week she lost her debit card, the next week her credit card, and somehow couldn't access her accounts online, so Zelda was always paying the bills and Heather had expensive tastes. She especially liked ordering all the appetizers on the menu and running up the check. So Zelda was having a bad week financially every month, then picking up extra shifts the other three weeks, not to mention that she wasn't working when Heather was in town. Zelda finally put her foot down and said that Heather had to start paying for stuff, about which Heather sort of played the victim card even though she had a lot of money.

Where was the money from? I asked. Heather freelanced, but there was also an older white guy, an alcoholic with an inheritance, who paid her to listen to him talk on the phone about his ex-wife and how messed-up his life was. He'd randomly drop a grand or two into her account, but she had to be on call all the time. Heather always upbraided him when he called, it's not like she was comforting or anything—he had to be some kind of masochist, Zelda inferred. I said it reminded me of the writer Anaïs Nin, who was famously commissioned to write custom-tailored pornography for a mysterious oil magnate—impecunious creative types have always done what they can to get by. Heather was also in hardcore psychoanalysis three times a week which didn't sound particularly affordable, rich alcoholic benefactor or not. But Heather had the sort of charisma that lets you talk your way into or out of anything, Zelda said, with a hint of either bitterness or nostalgia in her voice.

The two of them had been a thing for around six months. Being monogamous wasn't really a problem though Zelda thinks she's not monogamously inclined and had blown up her most serious previous relationship by cheating on her live-in girlfriend, whom I'd once met. But Heather took up so much emotional energy and so depleted her bank account it wasn't like there was mental space to have eyes for anyone else. Even so, Heather was super-jealous. She developed a fixation on the girl Zelda had dated previously and was still friends with, a YouTuber whose videos Heather would watch with an eagle eye, searching for obscure clues about her personality and demanding to know how many times she and Zelda were texting a month, and who Zelda thought was prettier, and counting the likes the YouTuber was getting on her photos and perorating at Zelda for having said Happy Birthday to her on Facebook.

In other words, theirs was a relationship entirely mediated by the internet, even when they were in the same room. Heather would be sitting next to Zelda on the couch, literally tweeting stuff Zelda had just said, or tweeting about how depressed and alone she was, and Zelda would be like, "Yo, I'm right here sitting next to you asking if you're okay!" Heather seemed to prefer the sympathy she got from Twitter, it seemed more vital to her emotional economy, though there was also never enough of it. There's no doubt that social media makes even us non-millennials into attention junkies—spilling it all online earns you those little gratification pellets ("likes," "influence," "attention"), and the creepiest element is how skillfully they've managed to implant those little kernels of surveillance capitalism right into the love-seeking parts of our psyches. The way the lovers actually *in the room* start seeming second best.

The first surveillance-themed reality TV show, the winkingly titled *Big Brother* (sure it's totalitarianism, but we'll make it fun) aired in the Netherlands, the birthplace of market capitalism, back in 1999, and fast became a worldwide franchise. In case you've forgotten, that was the one where a group of people live together in a big house, isolated from the outside world, continuously watched by television cameras. It turned out we love watching other people being watched.

The early crop of reality TV programs made being monitored seem like a path to glamour and fame obviously, but what's more interesting is the year of the debut. The surveillance aesthetic was becoming the cultural idiom in dominance even before the post-9/11 security state made succumbing to constant monitoring our patriotic duty; the cultural wing of the surveillance state was already in place well before the political justification was settled on.

At first it seemed like the people who went on reality TV were big narcissists and that casting directors were deliberately selecting annoying outsized personalities because that's what the genre needed: externalizers, attention-cravers, blurters. It turned out to be the perfect marriage of genre and character type, just as detective shows and Westerns had once demanded "inner-compass" types—loners and individualists who kept their own counsel and didn't need to be liked. Reality TV didn't *invent* narcissism obviously, it was a social type long on the rise as cultural scolds like Christopher Lasch and Tom Wolfe had been warning way back in the 1970s. But even in the 1950s social critics like David Riesman (*The Lonely Crowd*) were lamenting that the self was being eroded in ways that made us emptier and more docile. Did reality TV become so culturally dominant because these yearning personality types—craving attention and external validation—were already ascendant? Did digital capitalism help spawn them or did it just handsomely reward them? I'll leave the causality arrows to others. What I'm trying to get at is the way this confluence of forces—cultural, economic, political—conditions our most intimate moments, including how we love and are loved.

Sure, maybe Heather liked fomenting emotional chaos to have things to tweet about, but it's also the online ethos: grief-posting, tweeting about your sadness, saying things are hitting you harder than maybe they are in reality. She liked leaning over Zelda's shoulder when Zelda was on Twitter, commenting on what she was posting, as if there were no boundaries between the two of them, or none she could tolerate. There was a woman who was a regular at the place Zelda bartended and they'd tweet about random stuff, and Heather would be there reading the tweets saying, "Oh my god, you like her, do you like her?" Then she'd go to Zelda's profile and "favorite" all Zelda's tweets to the bar regular, as if to say "I see what you're doing!" And Zelda would be like, "I'm not *doing* anything!" It was this hyper-intimacy that Zelda got sucked into and thrilled to at first, but after a while it was becoming a neurotic cage.

Like a one-woman intelligence agency, Heather not only invaded Zelda's Twitter, she regularly went through her phone to glean intel (Zelda said she didn't know how Heather had gotten her password, though was less bent out of shape about it than I would have been). Heather wanted complete emotional transparency, reading Zelda's journals while she was at work, which led to further accusations: Zelda didn't like her anymore, Zelda had texted her cousins saying she needed Heather to leave. Which was disloyal!

Needless to say our phones make all of us transparent, they're diabolical location-tracking devices that happen to make calls, while storing your data for future law enforcement requests that your cellphone company will be more than happy to comply with. Why wouldn't our love lives conform to the same logic: our apps demand transparency, so too our lovers. The temptation to track a spouse's whereabouts isn't exactly uncommon (even in the old days suspicious spouses were foraging through desk drawers and credit card receipts). But the tenor of Zelda and Heather's relationship reminded me of going through a full body scanner at the airport—the first time I was outraged and wanted to kill the smirking TSA agent who commanded me to raise my arms and stand immobile while electromagnetic waves penetrated my body and shot through every orifice. Eventually, having to be transparent was just another travel inconvenience.

You can know all about social forces and still hold each other responsible for blurting and snooping. "Heather sounds good at weaponizing her anxieties," I said.

"She loves misery," Zelda replied.

Did Zelda get a little addicted to the drama too? I've been there, maybe you have also—hating the romantic chaos but finding yourself habituated to it and transfixed, unable to walk away. You're obligated to play shrink because they've dumped their problems on you, declared themselves patient-in-chief. You know they're in pain and you want to fix the pain; abandoning them would make you feel terrible about yourself. It was a familiar couple groove: Heather generated emotional pyrotechnics and hated that Zelda could step back from her feelings; she wanted what Zelda wouldn't give her, which was for Zelda to lose control too. Heather was like, I'm gonna throw your phone out the window or some other bit of bedlam-making, determined to make Zelda show some emotion one way or another. Which instead just left Zelda feeling cold, and scared of how much she felt like a robot.

Growing up playing the adult in a histrionic household had at least left Zelda with a useful emotional skill set: she knew how to deal with other people's volatility and projections. Though her parents lived apart and had never married, they were united in their unhappiness about her being queer (disapproving of her lifestyle, disapproving of her fade), which didn't seem to faze her terribly. Her mother, whom she'd discussed with me over the years, was anxious and reactive, her father she described as delusional, though she talked to them both frequently. So Zelda kept thinking she could make things *better* for Heather—get her to take her meds and calm down, then they could have a healthy relationship. If anyone could handle Heather it was her. She wasn't going to let Heather defeat her.

What *are* we allowed to expect from people in pain? Was Heather responsible for being such a difficult bitch, or was she a casualty of her psychology, not a moral agent but a sufferer? That was the dilemma. They'd both gotten in the habit of thinking of Heather as a victim—whether of bad brain chemistry or childhood trauma wasn't clear, but the language of trauma and PTSD is so embedded in our vocabulary of emotion these days, who can avoid it as a sense-making tool? Everyone in Zelda's sphere talked about their traumas and abuses with ease; even the dating apps condition you to spill your trauma before you've even *met* a potential mate, offering profile prompts like "What's your existential crisis?" Zelda said the new millennial dating cliché upon meeting someone new is asking "What's your toxic trait?" as an icebreaker, the millennial update on "What's your sign?" She didn't think it led to people revealing themselves in interesting ways, more like a lot of ragging about the last person they'd dated, and how they'd been wronged. She thinks the internet has made millennials boring. I informed her that people weren't all that interesting before the internet.

Hearing about all this mutual amateur psychoanalysis I was reminded of Wilhelm Stekel bemoaning, in his 1931 *Marriage at the Crossroads,* the tendency of overanalyzed people to start analyzing their mates, or what he calls the "analytic illness," and the predictably disastrous effects on their relationships. Stekel: "Both parties watch each other's every step and throw up to each other the desires of the unconscious.

The little symptomatic acts of daily life are cruelly dismembered and the forbidden wishes laid bare." Everyone should have the right to their own thoughts, yet in the analytic marriage—"perhaps the most unhappy of all marriages"—that goes by the wayside. "There must be realms of the soul which the mate can still discover with astonishment," advises Stekel. I very much wanted to send Heather to him for a consult. He relates the story of a married couple, both doctors, who jointly go into psychoanalysis, read a lot of books on the subject, and embark on a life of mutual faultfinding. The wife discovers "transferences" her husband has for his women patients; he deduces from her dreams that she's in love with one of his friends. Stekel steps in and forbids them all future analyzing if they want to save their relationship. "The first law of marriage is never to break into the soul of the beloved—never to penetrate into his soul's most hidden chamber of secrets."

Stekel was even more vehemently against transparency: "Truthfulness is no daily fare; it is the roughage of the psychotic person, destined to free him from his poisons and waste-products." (I imagine the association with toilets and shit is intentional.) Something of the unknown must always remain, even between two people in love.

On the opposing team was Heather: playing psychoanalyst was her avocation, but in a bloodthirsty way, Zelda thought, as if pathologizing Zelda helped her feel better about herself. Heather too was a world-class expert at employing online resources for interpersonal detective work, and her forays into Zelda's psyche included researching the most devastating thing that had happened to her: the death of her brother earlier that year, shot and killed by police after a family member reported that he'd shown up with a gun. Zelda was still grieving the loss.

Heather even managed to find the police bodycam footage of the shooting online, which she watched and insisted on describing to Zelda. She pored over the tapes of the 911 call, also online, describing the tonal inflection of the relative who'd made the call, despite Zelda saying she didn't want to know about it. Heather would stop for a while but then keep bringing it up, relating more fragments of information and what she'd deduced. Nothing was off-limits. Something in her needed to violate all boundaries, which seemed particularly monstrous to Zelda in this case. Her brother had been suicidal a lot of his life with manic episodes. I knew the phrase "suicide-by-cop," and from the details she related this seemed like a textbook case, abetted by the pattern of police in America shooting first and asking questions later when Black men are involved, though this was before George Floyd's death and sparked no international protests.

What was Heather after, probing into something so tragic? The pretense was "concern," but it felt sadistic to Zelda, like let's feel those painful things over and over. The demand seemed to be to merge completely, merge your pain, like you were floating together in an adult-sized womb. It got to the point that Zelda would shut down, then Heather would accuse her of withholding her feelings, the highest of crimes. Heather thought the kinds of therapy Zelda had had in the past—cognitive or behavioral—hadn't gotten to the root of her problems. Zelda's view was that Heather may have been getting to the root of something in psychoanalysis but was left constantly rehashing her trauma, and suffering more because of it, like she was eight years old going through everything again and again. Zelda accused Heather of thinking suffering was noble, like she needed it to be a great artist. It was an ongoing couple disagreement between them, but at a larger level also about whether a generation raised under the seductive sway of trauma theory can ever crawl out from under it.

The question of Blackness and how it plays out in relation to love came up occasionally in our conversations. Zelda thought it definitely makes a difference but wasn't sure exactly how. She observed that her straight Black women friends were less quick to put out than her white women friends, which she thought resulted from growing up with more sex negativity. There was always the residue of respectability politics to contend with—Zelda herself rarely swore I noticed, at least not with me, though maybe that was a teacher-student holdover. (Online she swore like a rapper.) Heather had grown up in a more unstable situation than Zelda's, raised by relatives in the projects because her mother was unstable. She hinted at childhood traumas and had scars, including physical scars, she wouldn't discuss, savoring her secrets while wanting Zelda's life to be an open book. Could Heather's emotional precarity be separated from the precarity of her family situation? Whatever the origin it ultimately made things between the two of them cataclysmic and impossible. But it was Heather who had a weird relation to her Blackness, Zelda thought, avoiding her Black friends when they were together, being awkward and uncomfortable around Zelda's family. This too was off-limits as a topic—when Zelda tried bringing it up, "It destroyed her world."

That seemed like a complicated conversation, I said—was it race or class being talked about? Zelda's family was middle class, her parents both college-educated. Black and middle class also meant a family of civil and public servants—an uncle who'd worked in the county prison system, which included guarding COVID-afflicted inmates, had recently died of COVID himself. When the family gathered for the funeral there was a lot of hugging, and a bunch of other relatives came down with it, though luckily no one had gotten as sick as her uncle. "Black people won't give up on the big send-offs no matter what," Zelda commented wryly.

As things between Heather and Zelda were winding down, they also got, predictably, crazier. Heather would book one-way flights and move in for weeks at a time. Zelda would have no idea when she was leaving. Finally she told Heather that she had to work and Heather had to go, and bought her a return ticket despite not being that flush herself. Heather managed to miss three flights in one week, and Zelda kept repurchasing tickets for her. The final straw came when Zelda woke Heather up at five a.m. for a flight and packed her suitcase for her; Heather was brushing her teeth when she looked at her phone and said, "Please don't be mad at me, but the flight was yesterday."

All this was painful to hear and made me feel protective of Zelda—I hated hearing about her working to pay someone else's bills. The relationship eventually ended for good when on another visit, Heather just wouldn't leave. She was FaceTiming people and saying Zelda was kicking her out, tweeting nasty things about her then deleting them, and creating so much chaos that Zelda finally left her own place for a couple of days, not knowing what she'd return to. Heather eventually cleared out (only some books were missing, which Heather always treated as communal property to Zelda's irritation), but even after the breakup the emotional hustling continued, like Heather calling at weird hours to say she'd just gotten attacked in a bar. Every day was another study in crisis: she couldn't get her meds or was upset the coffee shop was out of oat milk.

The good news was that lately Heather had been randomly sending five- or six-hundred-dollar chunks of restitution for the money Zelda had spent on her, or would buy Zelda something unnecessary, like a hoodie, then message on Twitter to ask if she'd gotten it. (She had to use Twitter because Zelda finally blocked her number after Heather texted fifty times in a row demanding to know why Zelda didn't love her and couldn't they try again.)

So Zelda was finally out of this protracted codependent thing, and now here was Heather's friend Tania requesting a convo with Olivia, and Heather calling up to make mischief again. Heather and Zelda talked, with Heather saying she wished Olivia and Zelda would just stop posting about each other and then none of this would happen, and Zelda pointing out that she couldn't tell someone what not to post on their own private page. (What did Tania want to say to Olivia, I wondered? It reminded me of *The Godfather*—Heather sending her consigliere to talk tough to potential rivals.)

And what was Olivia's response to all this? Zelda suspected that Olivia was flattered that people were reacting to her Finsta posts, and probably posting more because of the drama. So she likes Heather being jealous? "It definitely gave her a thrill I wasn't expecting," Zelda said, eyebrows signaling bemusement. And was Tania still on Olivia's Finsta? Yes. Leading Zelda to believe that some part of Olivia enjoyed Heather knowing stuff and being at the center of online conflagrations, and maybe that was a conversation they needed to have, like what are the boundaries for Finsta?

When I asked if some part of Zelda was attracted to conflagration too—after all, there did seem to be perpetual drama swirling around her—she said with interest, "Am I like that?" momentarily seeing herself from a foreign vantage which is always a jolt. Do the infinite possibilities for triangulation and psychodrama social media provides ratchet up people's desire levels, make things hotter? I tried to recall and recap for Zelda René Girard's theory in *Deceit, Desire and the Novel* that desire is always contagious, or as he puts it, "mimetic." We desire someone when someone else desires them. (Or desire them more—has it ever not been thus?) We're always *imitating* desire: it doesn't originate within us, it originates within this structure. We all want to be someone other than who we are, Girard thinks, and by desiring what someone else desires, the unconscious fantasy is that we'll be transformed into that person. It struck me that people were using the internet precisely this way almost incessantly: to promote desire's contagious properties. Hence all the conflict, or what Girard would call "mimetic rivalry," which always comes with an undercurrent of violence.

Zelda agreed that posting about people you were involved with invariably instigates conflict. There was this whole genre of people posting about their significant others then getting flurries of messages in response saying, "Hey, that's *my* significant other," or, "Take that down, he has a girlfriend." She'd literally seen women post about a boyfriend and instantly three other women would be posting, "Oh, this was him with me last night, and here's a photo of us." She had friends who'd been in relationships for years and never posted about it because you don't know what you'll find out. Even if the lover isn't cheating per se there's going to be flirting or provocative messages, which is inevitable because everyone's online all the time. Especially with straight men, it has to be less "Don't do it" and more like "Please don't embarrass me."

So it was guys who were mostly the cheaters? I queried. Not necessarily, but women were *better* cheaters, because women did better investigation work on the internet. Women were better at finding connections between people and knowing what will and won't come out. Men weren't as attuned to "who sees what" or what a retweet could mean, thus it was mostly men who are "figured out on the internet," Zelda explained. Though women could sometimes be pretty clueless too. She related an incident that happened at a club she'd once worked at. Patrons would be on Instagram or Facebook Live, which is where you post real-time videos of where you are. One night three women came in—paid *money* to get in, because there was a cover—wearing sweats and with their hair in ponytails, and marched directly to a specific section, like strictly business, and *beat this woman up,* and then just left. And everyone was like "Whoa, what just happened?" The internet happened—apparently she was with someone else's man and decided to advertise it in real time.

Growing up feeling like you're the star of your own reality show has left everyone so primed to spill everything on a moment-by-moment basis that Zelda says she sometimes has to stop mid-post to remind herself, "No, this does not go on the internet." But it feels like you've been socialized to be "that sort of person." She doesn't believe it's possible for anyone her age *not* to participate, at least she doesn't know anyone who's successfully kept secrets from the internet. Which left her swimming in clashing imperatives. Though an avid online forensic researcher, when she gets researched herself it feels like an intrusion. She objected to people googling and examining your social media—Facebook, Twitter, Instagram, LinkedIn, your personal website—then thinking they *know* you. She thinks it's invasive if a date asks about the photos of her first girlfriend on her page—"I'll tell you when I feel like it." Someone she met on Hinge started talking to her about her brother's killing, and Zelda thought, That's not a conversation we should be having yet! "Is there stuff about your brother on your Instagram?" I asked. Well yes, she'd posted photos of him.

Her theory is that there's a different type of narcissism with every type of social media user. The girl she was with before Heather, a makeup artist with a YouTube channel, was always taking selfies, always ready for her close-up and preoccupied with whether people were looking at her. She was actually a really nurturing person except that she needed to be on view all the time. But who doesn't? Even people my age bemoan the paucity of likes on a post, because attention has come to feel like a curative and a currency, a sign of your essential worth. Everyone's a celebrity with a coterie of fans following their every thought—even levelheaded

Olivia wanted her corner of Finsta stardom. If social media has democratized celebrity and everyone moves through the world in a gratifying bubble of publicity, it may be a curative but it's equally often a self-inflicted wound. Heather herself had not long before gotten thrown in the Twitter stockades for posting something she'd clearly thought was "edgy" and would garner the good kind of attention, but unfortunately the rest of her online world assessed it as criminally insensitive, so she'd quickly deleted it but not before someone screenshotted and reposted it, and a barrage of vicious online sadism came her way. When I checked her Twitter feed the screenshots were still up, with brutal comments by people telling her to go kill herself, which is not a great thing to tell a depressive. She'd blocked hundreds of followers and issued heartfelt apologias, but Twitter never forgets.

I occasionally wondered whether the millennial predilection for constant upheaval had something to do with the antidepressant intake, whether the general emotional tenor was so pharmaceutically muted that people needed extra jolts of stimulation to feel much of anything. I was recalling the eccentric Marxist psychoanalyst Wilhelm Reich about the effects of anorgasmia on the human personality, which was the key to all neurosis, he thought: when orgasms are bottled up, aggression and sadism result. It's a short step from bad orgasms to totalitarianism. I should add that Reich was also completely, as we now say, *heteronormative:* there are right and wrong ways those orgasms should be arrived at, and puny orgasms are as bad as none. Conversely, it was Freud's view, especially in his later years, that too *much* sexual liberalization would lead to social chaos—which can also be plausibly argued as regards our moment. Indeed, this was not so long ago the conservative consensus, until conservatives started paying their pool boys overtime to have sex with their wives while they watched, and swapping mates with their evangelical neighbors. (It's so-called progressives who've become the new puritans, but that's a longer sadder story.)

Compounding the drama, Zelda seemed to have an uncommon number of exes wanting things from her—it was practically a revolving door of exes. Lately one short-term paramour whom she'd met online, and who lived a couple of hours away, kept "dropping by"—this after they'd spent just one night together—claiming to be in town to see relatives. There was "too much urgency about it," Zelda complained, though she'd have "leaned into the crazy if she'd been more interesting."

Another ex had shown up at her place on Christmas bearing a banana pudding, saying, "Please eat this." This was Sabina, whom Zelda had also met online and moved in with after a couple of dates early on in the pandemic, cohabiting for six weeks during the stay-at-home orders. The problem was that Sabina was (nominally) straight, prompting Zelda's friends to tell her she had to stop dating straight girls—apparently this had happened before. But no one was working, so why not play house? The ambivalence "kept it interesting," Zelda said with a bit of a mock-heroism. Except she and Sabina kept having these conversations where Sabina would say she didn't see herself not ending up with a man, and Zelda finally put her foot down, saying, "Of course you should experiment, but there are only so many times I can be on the receiving end of this conversation because, like, *I am a person.*" (The way she said it reminded me of John Merrick in *The Elephant Man,* which I think I'd screened in one of the classes she'd taken with me.) This made Sabina upset, and she accused Zelda of being "all talk" when it came to fluidity.

After Zelda moved back to her own place and they hadn't spoken for a few weeks, Sabina called and confessed she'd had a threesome with two other women and been scared to tell Zelda, who said that was fine and that she, Zelda, had also slept with someone else, and Sabina asked who, and when Zelda told her Sabina started crying and going haywire, saying "How could you do this?" and Zelda said, "You literally had a threesome during a pandemic!" (Sabina subsequently got tested.) Zelda hadn't thought they were in something where they had to confess things to each other—no one had ever said anything about exclusivity.

She thinks the procession of returning exes has to do with her "giving too much"—she goes all out when she meets someone which raises expectations. Her cousins keep saying, "That's not casual dating, you always take it to the next level too fast!" Or: "Zelda, you just met this person and you're moving in already?" Now here was Sabina on Christmas saying she wanted to try again and that she'd messed up and

Zelda thought, *"No you're just lonely and you want to be back with me cooking your meals and drinking wine and playing chess,"* and she got that, but still thought the responsible thing was to part ways because they needed to ask themselves if they'd be together if there wasn't a pandemic, and the answer was probably no.

She thinks lesbians have a weird fixation about wanting to be friends with all their exes, while her straight friends are like, What is wrong with you, why do you still talk to that person? But she and the long-term ex she'd cheated on had watched a sappy lesbian Christmas movie together on FaceTime over the holidays and it was really nice, even though they didn't actually talk and weren't in the same room. But sometimes being with someone and not having to speak—even when virtual—can feel like the most wonderful intimacy.

CODA: ANTIBODIES

[Overheard on the internet mid-lockdown.]

My husband wanted to show me plots and graphs on a daily basis, I hate numbers and I'm especially angry about pie charts. My husband calls me a crypto-philistine.

My partner doesn't like the way the house is at the moment. I didn't like her commenting on it.

She thought the restrictions were ridiculous and were priming us all for a fascist takeover.

All the things that make me crazy after being together for thirty-four years were exacerbated. It made it crystal clear that he really is a slob, doesn't follow up on things, and so on. If I didn't know it then, I sure as hell know it now.

We had one very rough argument (for us), where the oven had a short and turned itself off, and my husband thought I had turned it off and was gaslighting him like his ex-wife would have. I got very upset and went outside until I could trust myself not to yell at him.

Spouse continued to sneak to the gym by keeping in personal contact with the owner and arranging appointments. Obviously causing tension because (1) it was illegal and (2) it was dangerous.

I hate that the TV is never off, that we only watch the shows that he likes and so I escape into my phone and he hates that.

He hates when I bring up the fact that women leaders are doing a better job navigating COVID and understanding the dangers.

I found it hard to live in a mental atmosphere of extreme paranoia that seemed immune to facts, e.g., about how little evidence there has been of contagion from surfaces.

He wanted to attend concerts, shrimp boils, move-in parties, and to make daily trips to Walmart (a sojourn sure to eviscerate any relationship). He in turn accused me of being sedentary and resembling his sister's stoner ex because I wouldn't leave the house. I became exhausted and indifferent.

There was tension from the fear of death and our fascist administration. My crankiness and despair gets on her nerves now and then. I can't say I blame her.

My spouse is upset that I washed my hands at the kitchen sink after coming from outside. I tried to remember but usually forgot. Sorry, not sorry.

He is clearly stressed with worry about the virus and less tolerant of any expression of stress on my part. A serious weakness in our relationship is that he is intolerant of my having negative feelings.

I was worrying he was never leaving the house at first and it was making him depressed but he agreed to take a walk in the morning each day.

My persistent anxiety about politics caused most of the fights. She doesn't disagree with me about the substance, but about how I have dealt with it, by drinking too much and loudly declaiming what I am upset about. She doesn't like when I raise my voice.

There were more conversations, but less intimacy and less sex.

Our relationship was already problematic as we've been drifting apart for years, but finances and health insurance prevent us from divorcing.

My husband tends to be more negative than I am. There were times when one of us would think we shouldn't talk about what we were thinking to give the other a break from the topics. There were times when I didn't want to hear anything negative, it's exhausting and I'd get annoyed. There were times when one of us would have a better day, and it would seem like the other would ruin it by focusing again on the negative things going on.

We've seen some shit during our time together, so we've had practice at gently coaxing one another off the ledge.

We stopped going to marriage therapy, first for quarantine reasons, also because it's too hard to deal with the emotional aspects. We barely interact beyond running the household. Now is not a good time to stir up drama.

Some days were better because he was less stressed. Some days were worse because he's still lazy as fuck.

It's clear that pretty much everything I do annoys the hell out of her. There have been periods when she's annoyed the hell out of me too. I'm the same person I was thirty years ago when we met—that might be the problem.

We have an open marriage, but we haven't been seeing our other partners at all. I miss my other partners, and I assume he does too, but we keep in touch. It's forced conversations we've never had.

More irritation, but also more partnership. We became too familiar with each other. Nobody could escape to school or an office. Eating and cooking every meal together became tiresome.

At first we got closer but now we fight constantly. We're sick of each other even though we love each other. We got lazy in terms of cooking, style, sex, flirting.

We've always spent a lot of time together, and we're kind of hermits, so not much has changed. There was increased anxiety over acceptable risks and increased lashing out, also thankfulness for having each other.

At first the shock made us more angry than we were ready for. A relationship that was hard became harder. Too late, you should have left him before, I said to myself. Now I'm just trapped, trying to see him as a roommate, a lover or just a friend, despite all the shit going on, including cheesy online sex and cheating.

It was very nice having more time together. More talking, in spite of work pressures.

My mental health went to shit. I believe he was suffering from compassion fatigue when I was sick. No time apart and juggling work plus kids suddenly at home instead of school created a lot of strain.

More watching of TV together and talking about it afterward. Slightly more sex.

I learned how hard it is for him to throw things out in general. I knew a little about this but now it has become very clear. If he gets a "good" rubber band from some kind of packaging or something, he saves it in this giant ball he has of rubber bands so he never has to buy them. Even throwing out takeout containers pains him.

It appears he has developed a drinking problem, possibly cheating, and god knows what else.

My lover got very depressed, took shit loads of booze and pills, stopped communicating for a while and put on fifteen pounds. I lost eight pounds, got fit, reclaimed a garden and wrote some fiction.

She's become quite a pothead. Which is funny and not a problem. And she's lazy as heck.

He counts out how many berries he eats for breakfast. And before you ask, twelve blackberries, or eighteen blueberries.

She's more fearful about death than I'd thought. Her devotion to her father is admirable but I could also do with less of it.

He turns out to have major control issues. If I do the wash and fold his underwear, I'll find him refolding it before he puts it away. Even after he showed me precisely how he likes it folded and complimented me on my jockey-folding skills.

The man really likes bourbon and can drink a lot of it way too fast.

He has a weird neurosis about checking the doors are shut and the stove is off before we go to bed, and it's gotten a bit more pronounced since COVID.

He's fun to be with and laughs at my jokes. Which is everything.

He's more fond of hand sanitizer than I would have predicted.

His video game addiction went over the top.

He's more of a hypochondriac than I am. He thought he had COVID many times based on minor (though weird if real) symptoms.

She tends to be pollyannaish and optimistic while compartmentalizing bad things.

We're drinking a lot more wine than before.

I learned the depth of his anxiety and the substance of his insecurity in ways I hadn't ever known.

I never thought he'd have sex online with some work colleague while I'm in the other room . . . and still deny that he did something wrong.

My partner knows way more about the NBA and its players than I would have thought.

We're each perfectly fine people. We just don't have a lot in common.

When we get around to having sex it's good and we're like, "Hey we should do that more."

We've been having more sex and more varied sex—never underestimate the hunger of a man approaching pension age.

Sex was worse at the beginning of lockdown . . . then we probably panicked and wanted to fuck like there's no tomorrow . . . it was a bit crazy. Until she got a dog. The sex stayed good but got less frequent. Thanks to the dog, no more spontaneous couch sex.

Sex got worse since we're not seeing other people, even if intimacy probably improved. But maybe having sex with other people makes it more exciting to have sex with your own partner?

We're coworkers now. We go to bed at the same time as the kids. We fight less because we're ridiculously diplomatic and don't raise contentious issues or stick to our guns on anything.

We have certain problems because of our different opinions about sexual freedom: I'm more of a libertine, which creates tension. We don't believe in monogamy, but I'm more attracted to sexual freedom than he is.

Our sex life definitely suffered because of too much together time. The scales are tipping toward lifelong asexuality.

Being stressed out about money made me have to up my antidepressant dosage which seems to have killed my libido. Or maybe it was the stress that killed it. Either way I'm rarely in the mood anymore and sexual contact just feels jostling.

I've been wishing I could come out to my wife about my extramarital sexual relationships. I'd like a polyamorous marriage. But COVID life made opening that can of worms seem ill advised.

Sex has always been good, but the surrounding gloom definitely damaged our libidos.

My patience for being monogamous is wearing a little thin.

We'd been having issues with our sex life—to the point where it led to poor decisions on my part that made us seek couples therapy.

Seeing him stressed out and upset was a turnoff.

Pandemic sex was better at first, until he misplaced the pot. Then it wasn't better, just good.

It's frustrating living with someone you adore but who isn't sexual. But he's the best partner in every other way. If I could I'd look for a lover but that's not exactly possible at the moment.

He thought that I was using COVID as an excuse to not have sex after I read an account of someone not getting COVID even though their partner had because they properly distanced, and I figured we should keep our distance since he was working in a risky environment with people who weren't being reasonably careful. And maybe I was using it as an excuse. (I think I probably was to some degree.)

Our sex life got better on the whole because there's been more time for it. I also wonder if feeling like the species might be in danger gets libidos going.

I used to compare him to other partners and think about how even though I love him and am attracted to him, there were others I had better sex with. Now I thank my lucky stars every day that the person I'm stuck with is him.

I've been sneaking away to see lovers (all have had COVID fortunately and show antibodies) but my ability to get out of the house undetected has been diminished.

I think it's more important to find a partner you can get along with and communicate with effectively than one who stokes deep passions and poetic longing. My partner was someone I was deeply, hopelessly in love with (and still am), but we're so incredibly different. COVID laid bare just how difficult those differences really are.

Now that you were literally stuck in place, you had to make peace with your compromises. Which made me a lot more pessimistic.

I've always known that people need some distance to feel love, and certainly lust. But the quarantine proved it to me again.

COVID found me with a housemate in NYC while my lover thirty miles away sheltered with his wife. I wanted to be with him even more than before and found the inability to be the one to help ensure his safety intolerably painful.

Marriage is a crappy institution that chains lower-income folks to one another. The fact that healthcare is tied to employment in the U.S. makes it worse.

I worry that large swaths of society cannot love each other, but my relationship with my wife is solid. She's the little bit of the future that I can still imagine.

Lockdown made me very lonely, it made me realize how empty my life has been.

I miss physical contact, the smell of a woman's hair, the way they laugh (my wife is not much when it comes to humor, or at least my humor).

Any of us could be dead in two weeks. Any of us could be hospitalized or dead tomorrow. Tell the people you love that you love them.

Love is about being there for each other. It's about adjusting to each other's personalities. Being able to allow differences, and sometimes rein yourself in for someone else. I don't mean in a bad way, or all the time. I mean by having consideration about how you affect others.

COVID brought about a set of circumstances that made me realize how very selfish one of the most selfless people I've ever known (my spouse) really was.

Seeing all the pictures of people suffering, imagining my husband could be one of them, has made me more sensitive to his needs and opened my heart more. And I think his feelings toward me have gotten more generous. I think our love has grown in the direction of empathy.

Our love isn't the romantic lovey-dovey kind—except when it needs to be. It's something resilient and wide and it makes me laugh at how most people define love.

I'd spent so much time (years) thinking about what our love doesn't look like, but quarantining allowed me to see what it actually looks like, and I'm here for it. So much.

COVID gave me a deadly taste of the despair of loneliness. The embargo imposed upon human touch and closeness by COVID was repugnant to me. The fact that people would go out with their faces covered with masks took away the charm of going out. It started to feel like there was an unbridgeable distance among human beings.

I don't know if other people are going through the same sort of existential reflection, but contemplating mortality and facing so much uncertainty has put an emphasis on love (in this one life we get) as worth protection and sacrifice.

We're grateful every day for the presence of each other in our lives.

Our relationship requires a social village more than I realized. One person isn't "enough" for me.

COVID made me realize that love is transformative in ways I didn't think possible. At my age, I expected us to both be set in our ways, but being forced to rely on one another showed me how much passion is still available for us.

Maybe love is banal, but banal is what's needed sometimes.

ACKNOWLEDGMENTS

I'm deeply grateful to all the roving consultants and fellow sufferers who shared their stories of love and contagion with me, including everyone who responded anonymously to the online questionnaire I posted about coupled conditions under lockdown. I've benefited from the kindness of many strangers.

Thank you to those who braved chapters in progress: Anna McCarthy, Val Monroe, Alice Entin, Myra Balesi, Len Kipnis, Phyllis Kipnis, Nancy Goodman, Lani Goodman, and my agent PJ Mark. And thanks to Amana Fontanella-Khan and Ian Buruma, my editors at *The Guardian* and *The New York Review of Books,* where some of these ideas were first essayed.

Bruce Robbins is always my most meticulous and encouraging reader. At a crucial moment Adam Ross gave me a hard-hitting yet inspirational talking-to about devilishness versus reportage, which helped hugely.

It was a pleasure and a privilege to have Erroll McDonald,

my editor on *Against Love,* edit my latest foray into the subject. Someone once called him an evil genius (it was probably me), but the fact is he's merely a genius.

Thank you especially to my most treasured interlocutor and cellmate.

A NOTE ABOUT THE AUTHOR

Laura Kipnis is a cultural critic and former video artist whose work focuses on sexual politics, aesthetics, shame, emotion, acting out, moral messiness, and various other crevices of the American psyche. Her previous seven books have been translated into fifteen languages. Kipnis is a professor at Northwestern University, where she teaches filmmaking. Her writing has appeared in *The New York Review of Books, The Guardian, Slate, The Atlantic, Harper's Magazine, Playboy, The New York Times Magazine, The New York Times Book Review,* and *Bookforum.* She lives mostly in New York.

A NOTE ON THE TYPE

The text of this book was set in Sabon, a typeface designed by Jan Tschichold (1902–1974), the well-known German typographer.

Typeset by Scribe
Philadelphia, Pennsylvania

Printed and bound by Berryville Graphics
Berryville, Virginia

Designed by Michael Collica